CAMBRIDGE STUDIES IN CRIMINOLOGY, VOLUME XXVII
Editor: Sir Leon Radzinowicz

SUSPENDED SENTENCE

THE HEINEMANN LIBRARY OF CRIMINOLOGY
AND PENAL REFORM

CAMBRIDGE STUDIES IN CRIMINOLOGY

XIX *Murder followed by Suicide*, D. J. West
XX   *Borstal Reassessed*, R. Hood
XXI *Crime in England and Wales*,
     F. H. McClintock and N. H. Avison
XXII *Delinquency in Girls*,
     J. Cowie, V. Cowie and E. Slater
XXIII *The Police: a Study in Manpower*,
     J. Martin and Gail Wilson
XXIV *Present Conduct and Future Delinquency*, D. J. West
XXV *Crime, Law and the Scholars*, G. O. Mueller
XXVI *Principles of Sentencing*, D. A. Thomas
XXVII *Suspended Sentence*, M. Ancel
XXVIII *Social Consequences of Conviction*,
     J. Martin and D. Webster
XXIX *Local Prisons: the Crisis in the English Penal System*,
     R. Sparks

SUSPENDED SENTENCE

A report presented by
The Department of Criminal Science
of the Institute of Comparative Law, University of Paris

under the direction of

Marc Ancel

Presiding Judge of the Supreme Court of France
Member of the Institut de France

to
The Cambridge Institute of Criminology

HEINEMANN
LONDON

Heinemann Educational Books Ltd
LONDON EDINBURGH MELBOURNE TORONTO
AUCKLAND SINGAPORE JOHANNESBURG
HONG KONG NAIROBI IBADAN NEW DELHI

ISBN 0 435 82020 6

© The Cambridge Institute of Criminology 1971

First published 1971

Publisher's note: This series is continuous with the Cambridge Studies in Criminology, Volumes I to XVIII, published by Macmillan & Co, London

Published by
Heinemann Educational Books Ltd
48 Charles Street, London W1X 8AH
Printed in Great Britain by
Morrison and Gibb Ltd, London and Edinburgh

Contents

Foreword *by Sir Leon Radzinowicz*	vi
Preface	ix
1. Origins	1
2. The Conditional Sentence from the Legal Standpoint	20

    The Basic Principles of the Institution
    Conditions for Granting a Suspended Sentence
    The Effects of the Conditional Sentence

3. The Geographical Spread of the Suspended Sentence	38

    Historical Background
    Present Systems
    The Technique of the Suspended Sentence
    Operational Period
    Obligations Imposed
    The Granting of a Suspended Sentence
    Revocation
    The Effects of a Suspended Sentence
    The Application of the Suspended Sentence

4. Judicial Practice and the Results of the Suspended Sentence	53

    The use of the Suspended Sentence by Different Jurisdictions
    The Results of the Suspended Sentence

Comparative Conclusions	65
Statistical Appendix	73
Index	100

Foreword

by

Sir Leon Radzinowicz

THE suspended sentence, so recently introduced into this country, is already facing an acute crisis of confidence. If the trend of evidence on its results is not swiftly reversed it may soon be on its way out here. The crux of the matter is that it was included in the Criminal Justice Act 1967 because it was intended to do good. It was hoped that it would reduce the mounting pressure on the prisons by cutting down the number of short sentences served. It was also hoped that it would make it easier for courts to reserve probation for those in real need of that kind of treatment.

Now it is being said, and said with some vehemence, that just the opposite is taking place. The suspended sentence, it is claimed, is contributing indirectly to the increase in short-term imprisonment: it is acting as an accelerator rather than a brake. By employing a suspended sentence rather than a fine, a court restricts its own future discretion. Where a suspended sentence has been imposed, a specific threat has been made, and in the event of a further offence, there is little option but to put that threat into execution. Nor can any beneficial effect, direct or indirect, be demonstrated by way of compensation for this signal defeat of the main purpose of the new measure. It is cold comfort to be told by a government spokesman that he has been told by the statisticians that the size of the prison population is much the same as it would have been had the suspended sentence not been introduced.[1] It is a little like having a set of dentures which do not ache but do not bite either.

The adoption of the suspended sentence in this country was, indeed, based more upon a pious hope than upon examination of hard evidence. In 1952 the Advisory Council on the Treatment of Offenders, though presided over by Lord Birkett who was certainly no enemy of innovation, decisively rejected a proposal to introduce the suspended sentence here. With the growing urgency of the search for alternatives to short terms of imprisonment, the Advisory Council looked at it again in 1957, without finding any reason to reverse that verdict. Indeed, we reproduced in our report the statement by our forerunners, setting out the reasons for rejection. A not untypical specimen of our isolationism is that the only available source of evidence about the working of suspended sentences—their use and development in the countries which originated or adopted them—was never examined in detail and still remains largely unknown.

The suspended sentence is essentially a continental system. It began its meteoric career over seventy years ago, with the Belgian and French

[1] See statement by Lord Windlesham, in House of Lords Debate on 'Overcrowding in Prisons', *Hansard*, 2 Dec. 1970, col. 556.

laws of 1888 and 1891, these marked an important and humane innovation, for the first time weakening, if not breaking the iron equation of crime and punishment affirmed by the classical codes. From there it has made a *tour du monde*. Before the end of the nineteenth century it had ventured into Norway and Portugal and a mutation in the shape of a 'pardon' had appeared in parts of Germany. Before the first world war, whilst England was turning to probation, it had swept most of the rest of Western Europe. In addition it had gone as far afield as Egypt, Japan, and most of the countries of Latin America. After the war it surged over Eastern Europe—Finland, Russia, Czechoslovakia, Rumania and Poland. It eventually reached Israel (which already had probation) in 1954, before entering the United Kingdom, as a very late immigrant, in 1967.

Not only has the suspended sentence travelled widely, it has assumed many different national costumes on the way, as well as adapting itself to changes in penal fashion over the years. It has been scrutinised by administrative experts and learned bodies, it has been debated in parliaments, it has been clothed in various legislative guises. A few countries, such as Spain, Greece, Italy and most of the Latin American States, still cling to the virgin simplicity of the original suspended sentence, though even some of them are casting wistful glances in the direction of probation, its more adventurous and adaptable sister. Most countries have already permitted their courts to use one or more devices derived from probation as alternatives, or in addition to, the suspended sentence. Very commonly a regime of supervision or rehabilitation can now accompany suspension. In some countries the imposition of the sentence can be suspended, and not merely its enforcement. Belgium itself now permits any permutation of suspension and supervision. France and Western Germany allow either the ordinary suspended sentence or that with supervision added. Israel, since 1963, allows either probation or suspended sentence, or the two combined. In some countries where the suspended sentence remains on the statute books, it has been ousted in practice by variations or probation, such as the community supervision favoured by socialist states like Russia. Elsewhere it may be probation that remains unused or under-used, for lack of adequate supervisors.

Even today, however, this rich variety of foreign experience remains largely unknown in England. In view of this, and of the growing doubts about the use of the suspended sentence here, I thought it desirable to put before the British public a critical study of the working of this institution elsewhere. I approached Monsieur Marc Ancel—Presiding Judge of the Supreme Court of France, Member of the Institut of France, a penologist of international reputation, and a long-standing friend of the Cambridge Institute—to take charge of the preparation of such a report, embracing experiences from all over the world. We are indeed grateful to him and to his collaborators for this rich and informative piece of comparative evidence.

The first thing that the English-speaking reader will notice is that the suspended sentence has been, in a sense, a poor relation of probation, more limited in the circumstances of its birth and confined during its early years—and to some extent still—by a more rigid legal system. This in itself is relevant to the growing discussion of the continuation of the measure in this country.

A second rather startling feature that emerges is the poverty not only of firm evidence as to the effectiveness of the suspended sentence, but even of official statistics from which such evidence could be derived. It is particularly strange that in France—the country which once took the lead in the development of criminal statistics—figures showing the number of suspensions revoked each year ceased to be kept after 1930. Similarly in Israel—where some attempts have been made at systematic assessments of effectiveness—it is admitted that the proportion of suspended sentences activated each year is not known, and that research is still needed on such crucial problems as whether allowing courts more discretion about enforcement has increased the number of breaches of suspended sentences, whether it has reduced general deterrence, how the 'success' of suspended sentences compares with that of probation, what is the effect of combining it with probation.[1]

Judging from all this, criminological assessment of the effectiveness of this measure is still rudimentary and inconclusive. The fundamental question still remains unanswered. Where there is available conditional discharge, probation, fine—and sometimes, almost inevitably, short-term imprisonment—the only justification there could be for adding suspended sentence to the range is that it would more effectively prevent further delinquency. And this, like most of the other assumptions about the suspended sentence, is so far quite unproven.

I personally feel that the days of the suspended sentence in England are numbered.[2] But the interest of this monograph is more permanent, recording as it does a fascinating chapter in the penal history of the world. The Institute has indeed been fortunate in securing the co-operation of Monsieur Ancel in making it available to those in this country who are concerned to understand and to weigh all possible devices for dealing with offenders.

The manuscript was delivered to us in French, and I should like to pay tribute to the work of the translator, Mrs Judith Chambers. I should also like to acknowledge the valuable editorial help received from Miss J. F. S. King.

We welcome the book as a distinguished addition to the Cambridge Series.

Cambridge
December 1970

[1] See Leslie Sebba, 'Penal Reform and Court Practice: The Suspended Sentence', in the impressive volume *Studies in Criminology* (1969) edited by Professor I. Drapkin S. on behalf of the Criminological Institute, Hebrew University of Jerusalem, pp. 133–170.
[2] See *The Sunday Times*, 17 January 1971, which includes Mr Lewis Chester's inquiry and my comments.

Preface

FOR nearly a century penologists and legislators on the continent have been preoccupied with the question of the conditional sentence, or the suspension of the execution of a sentence. Although for a long time this measure was seen as being in contradistinction to the probation system, at one stage it seemed possible that the two might be merged. However, despite this, the continental countries have all kept their own variations of the suspended sentence, even while incorporating some elements from the probation system. There has been a renewal of interest in the last few years, because of the system instituted by the Swedish Penal Code in 1962, and the adoption of the suspended sentence by England herself in 1967. At this stage, therefore, it would be useful to have a general examination of this subject. However, the difficulties presented by such a project are threefold.

First, the exact origins of the conditional sentence are extremely uncertain. In our first chapter we shall try to establish that the practice dates back to a measure which was in force at the end of the nineteenth century and that it belongs, basically, to the Franco-Belgian legal system. There has been much argument about this, and the controversy has sometimes tended to obscure both the recent and early origins of the suspended sentence.

Rather more serious are those difficulties relating to the precise definition, or characterization, of the suspended sentence. Because even if we accept that it was first established in Belgium in 1888 and then in France in 1891, it has undergone many changes since then. In order to define it, we must be sure which system of suspended sentence we are dealing with: is it the one which was operating in 1888, or that in force in continental legislation in 1968? Also, we must decide whether we mean suspended sentence as the written law of the continental countries has it, or as it is practised in the courts, or as seen from the doctrinal, theoretical or penological point of view. Consequently, there is risk of confusion if we do not make it clear which form of suspended sentence we are discussing. All of them must be considered, but we must be sure to distinguish them as we go along.

The third kind of difficulty relates to the actual working of the conditional sentence. We have mentioned (and will take the point up again later on) that in practice the suspended sentence can sometimes appear quite different from its written definition in the statutes. So, what might be called a sociological study of actual applications would be useful. Unfortunately, as we shall see, the information on this is very difficult to obtain, at least in a scientific and objective way. Statistics are either inadequate or deceptive, because an overall figure for suspended sentences at any one time in a given country is not in itself significant, since it tells us only for which offences, and not to which offenders, the sentences have been applied. Moreover, suspended sentence with *mise à l'épreuve*[1] derived from probation, is gradually being adopted on the continent alongside the simple suspended sentence laid down in 1888 and 1891. The available figures usually lump together all the different types of suspended sentence and do not distinguish the intermediate forms, so that here again statistical comparison could be deceptive.

We decided, despite all these difficulties, that it was still possible to undertake this study, but it has been necessary to limit it. To try to discuss all the systems of conditional sentence at present in operation in every country in Europe seems illusory and impracticable and would in any case require longer research. Then again, it would be pointless to discuss at length all the intermediate forms between suspended sentence proper and probation, as we can always refer to a well-known United Nations study on this subject. Neither have we tried to present a sociological or juridico-psychological study such as we referred to above. The results of research on this score seemed too inconclusive to be presented as a scientific survey. So, although we have no intention of neglecting the sociological and psychological point of view, we are confining ourselves to a complete study of the working of the institution on the French or Franco-Belgian model, at the same time touching on certain other facts which we have been able to obtain and verify.

The object and scope of this book should now be clear: we are attempting to disentangle and to analyse the suspended sentence as a legal institution and as a sociological-legal device for combating the phenomenon of crime. To this end we have first traced the origins of the conditional sentence and then tried to establish its full significance as a legal measure, which seemed to us essential for an understanding of the socio-legal problem. We have tried to show clearly with what results and with what success the measure has been applied, in France in particular. We have also outlined the international development of the suspended sentence because, having retraced its history, we felt it necessary to put it into what might be called its geographical context. Finally, we have drawn some general conclusions on a threefold level—comparative, juridical and sociological.

We would like to thank Miss Yvonne Marx, Maître de Recherche au Centre National de la Recherche Scientifique, Miss Denyse Chast, Assistant au Centre Français de Droit Comparé, and Mr Jacques Verin, Magistrat au Ministère de la Justice, as well as Miss Monique Robichon, Assistant au Centre Français de Droit Comparé, for their effective collaboration.

---

[1] *Translator's note:* Mise à l'épreuve is similar to probation in some respects (especially in that the offender is under supervision), but it is not identical with probation and therefore the French term has been retained wherever it is used in the original.

I

Origins

To seek out the origins of the suspended sentence involves asking three kinds of question and taking a stand at different points in time. Though it might seem logical to examine the proposals set out in the Bérenger and Lejeune Acts and to detect in their formulation the direct derivation of the Franco-Belgian system, such an examination would nevertheless be inadequate. We have only to read the law reports to see that to deal with certain offences by a conditional sentence was not a totally new idea even then. The researches of jurists, and especially of penologists, concerned with the problem of short-term imprisonment, the increase in recidivism and the possible link between the two, had nearly always resulted in advocacy of a system called 'conditional sentence'. Therefore, while not wishing to deprive Senator Bérenger of the authorship of an institution which is often called 'the Bérenger Act', we must point out that the idea had been in the air for some time.

Discussions of the subject which have appeared in the proceedings of various penitentiary congresses and in the works of certain writers should also be included in the origins of the suspended sentence.

Lastly, there are the remote antecedents of the institution, apparently undreamed of by the instigators of the 1891 law, and which commentators on this law seem to have tried *a posteriori* to discover.

We are going to examine all of these in chronological order, discussing first the historical antecedents of the suspended sentence, secondly its early beginnings and lastly its direct derivations.

THE HISTORICAL BACKGROUND

Many writers studying and commenting on the French law of 1891 and the introduction of the suspended sentence, attempt to attribute its origins to ancient French, or even to old Anglo-Saxon law.

1. The penal law of the *ancien régime*, with its numerous penalties, also recognized various moral sanctions, or means of mitigating, and even of revoking, penalties imposed. These historical precedents can be compared with the measure introduced into French law by the Bérenger Act. Thus there was admonition, a moral penalty consisting of a reproof delivered by the judge to the offender, warning him not to commit the same offence again under pain of more serious punishment. This very ancient penalty[1] was adopted by canon law under the name of *monitio* or *censura*, while secular law had two forms of admonition, differing in gravity: admonition proper, which we have mentioned above, for minor offences, and reprimand, a more serious type of admonition, with restricted application.

This benevolent measure which, like suspension, avoided the infliction of a more serious punishment, had certain advantages in that it allowed minor offences to be dealt with by a simple warning. It thus made possible the effective grading of penalties and, while not leaving the offender unpunished, it kept him from the pernicious influence of prison. The aim of this type of penalty was not only to punish the offender by the shame of being reproved in open court, but also to correct him and to warn him to change his way of life, Domat stated perceptively. The value of admonition was further recognized in the nineteenth century when several foreign legislatures adopted it.[2] And a professor of criminal law in the University of Modena[3] expressed the following appreciation of the institution: 'This measure of admonition is one of the innovations in the Sardinian Penal Code on which the justiciary of this country should congratulate

---

[1] In the Digest it is called *severa interlocutio*.
[2] Among the legislation which established judicial reprimand were: Article 41 of the Code of the Two Sicilies, Article 13 of the Turkish Code, Article 24 of the Spanish Code; the Portuguese Penal Code of 1852 and the Bavarian Penal Code of 1853.
[3] Ludovico Bosellini.

ORIGINS 3

themselves, and one which should figure in the penal law of every civilized nation'.¹

Bonneville de Marsagny, in France, shared the Italian writer's view and wanted this measure to be re-established in French penal law: 'The influence of the penal laws will be considerably enhanced when this simple judicial admonition achieves, in the eyes of all, the status and effectiveness of a punishment'.²

As well as judicial reprimand, other ancient institutions are mentioned by writers as possible ancestors of present-day suspension. There were the letters of favour, which depended on the benevolence of the sovereign and which were divided into letters of pardon, letters of abolition and letters of commutation of sentence. Certain writers have chosen to see pardon as a forerunner of the suspended sentence, pointing out the similarities which may exist between the two institutions. But it is more precise to say that the suspended sentence, like pardon, 'depends on the same concept of penal law: the idea of a criminal policy substituted for the idea of expiation'.³

Still other writers cite an institution written into the Etablissements de Saint Louis in the thirteenth century, and the charters of certain communes in Northern France. This was *asseurement*, defined by Esmein as 'the solemn promise given by one person to another to abstain from all violence towards him. This promise, once given, could not be withdrawn, and if it was broken, such violation constituted a capital crime.'⁴

However, while links can be detected between the suspended sentence and the institutions cited above, the differences must also be considered. Admonition specified that there should be a penalty for further commission of the same offence, but the penalty itself was not fixed. Furthermore, it applied only to minor offences. The letters of favour depended on the sovereign; they did not issue from the judge and laid down neither penalties nor conditions. As for *asseurement*, this was hardly ever used as a

---

[1] Quoted in Bonneville de Marsagny, *De l'amélioration de la loi criminelle*, 1864, p. 236.
[2] Bonneville de Marsagny, *op. cit*, p. 235.
[3] M. Oudinot, 'L'application de la loi de sursis en France', *Bull. de l'Union intern. de droit. pén.*, Vol. 18, Berlin, 1911, p. 70.
[4] Quoted by Dubois, *Les 'asseurements' au XIIIe siècle dans nos villes du Nord*, 1900.

preventive measure. It was a special undertaking referring to violence against a specific person, and not a general undertaking to be of good behaviour,[1] and the idea of the conditional suspension of punishment following an offence is not included in it at all.

2. If it is difficult to talk of antecedents of the suspended sentence in the ancient French legal institutions, it would certainly be an exaggeration to think that the Bérenger and Lejeune Acts found their source in foreign law. However, we shall mention certain non-French institutions which may have a bearing on the matter.

It might be asked whether the recognizance, through probation, has not had an influence on the evolution of the suspended sentence. We know that the recognizance consists of 'obliging persons who, it is feared, will commit offences in the future, to declare and give assurance publicly that they will *not* be guilty of such offences as are anticipated'.[2] Although basically a preventive measure, this was applied very early on in a punitive way.

We would quote further the practices of certain courts. In the fourteenth century, the ecclesiastical courts used a kind of suspended sentence. In the fifteenth and sixteenth centuries the courts of Zurich applied a similar kind of traditional suspension, allowing the offender to go free with the threat of more serious punishment in case of relapse. This measure was usually accompanied by conditions and prescriptions of behaviour. Hungarian judicial practice was similar in the sixteenth and seventeenth centuries.[3] In Sweden, before 1734, it happened quite often that the court warned the offender and exempted him from any penalty for the offence committed, threatening him with the original sentence if it was committed again. This practice was abandoned after the introduction of the 1734 Penal Code.[4]

It is interesting to note that these different institutions or jurisprudential practices were being applied and developed at a time when the arbitrary powers of the judge would seem to render

---

[1] Cf. Roland Berger, *Le système de probation anglais et le sursis continental*, pp. 14–15.
[2] Blackstone, *Commentaries on the Laws of England*, Vol. IV, p. 251.
[3] Cf. Roland Berger, *op. cit*, p. 15.
[4] Cf. I. Strahl, 'Les Sanctions' in *Le droit pénal des pays scandinaves*, Paris.

their use pointless and superfluous. No doubt it appeared to the judge of the *ancien régime* that, far from restricting his powers, such measures offered the possibility of varying the method of repression of an offence while enabling him to exercise his arbitrary choice of sentence.

It should come as no surprise to find no trace of these supposed forerunners of suspension in the new statutes at the French Revolution. The reason for their disappearance is twofold: first, the suppression of the judge's arbitrary power, which had become intolerable through frequent abuse; the replacement of this power by the principle of strict legality of penalties excluded the granting of suspension or any similar measure. In fact, in drawing up the 1791 Penal Code, the Constituent Assembly was guided by the principle that 'it is essential that there be nothing obscure, uncertain or arbitrary in the ideas which evolve concerning offences and penalties . . . the criminal code cannot be too precise'.[1] This new conception, according to which the Code was omnipotent and omniscient, while the judge was relegated to the role of 'automatic dispenser' of penalties[2] was certainly hostile to the idea of the suspended sentence or any similar measure.

But it is the second reason which absolutely precluded its acceptance in the new criminal policy put forward by the Revolutionary legislature: the fact that deprivation of liberty was held in such high favour as a punishment by the authors of the 1791 Penal Code. Prison seemed to them to be the ideal punishment, since it contributed, in their eyes, to the effective protection of society and to the improvement of the offender. The utopian nature of such a concept can no doubt be explained by the novelty that surrounded the introduction of 'prison as a punishment' into the French legal system.

In fact, the penal law of the *ancien régime* had recognized prison as a penalty only in exceptional cases. The sanctions which had existed in the old law were essentially corporal punishments, which were often very brutal. Traditionally imprisonment had been used simply for the custody or detention of offenders until

---

[1] Marat, *Plan de législation criminelle*, 1790, pp. 27 and 28.

[2] In one of his reports to the Constituent Assembly, Lepelletier de Saint-Fargeau defined the role of the magistrate as follows: 'He must look into the law and find a punishment which is precisely applicable to the known facts. His only duty is to pronounce such penalty.' (P.V. *tome* 57, pp. 11 and 12.)

such time as they could conveniently be dealt with. The consensus among penologists of the period was that prisons were made *ad continendos non ad puniendos homines*.[1]

Under the old régime, then, prison did not in itself constitute a punishment. Consequently, the question of granting suspension of loss of liberty did not arise. For the idea of a conditional sentence to evolve, it was necessary not only that a repressive measure of loss of liberty should be written into French law, but that it should have functioned for a certain length of time. It was a case of stepping back far enough to evaluate the advantages and disadvantages of a particular penalty and of considering the influence of a term in prison on men who were one day to be restored to the community. Then there was the problem of rehabilitation of offenders, which gradually came to be seen as the main purpose of the punishment. The institution of the suspended sentence would be a way in which this aim could be achieved, since it could be defined as 'a sentence which does not degrade'.[2]

But it is only by delving back into the early beginnings of the idea of the suspended sentence that we will see these new problems in perspective.

THE EARLY BEGINNINGS

Nineteenth-century penology in France, alarmed by the increase in crime and above all in recidivism, began to question the usefulness of punishment in general and in particular the penalty of loss of liberty. The conclusion was that prison more often than not had a detrimental effect on the offender, and that a remedy must be found for the injurious nature of imprisonment. Out of this arose firstly the idea of the 'alternative sentence' and secondly that of the conditional suspension of prison sentences.

Three closely linked ideas dominated legal writing at the time and provided material for discussions at penitentiary congresses. Firstly there was the wish to avoid prison sentences, which were thought to be injurious, especially for first offenders. Then,

---

[1] Muyart de Vouglans, *Instruction criminelle suivant les lois et ordonnances du Royaume*, 1767, p. 255.
[2] Saleilles, *L'individualisation de la peine*, 2nd edn. 1909, p. 176.

ORIGINS 7

and partly linked with this, there was concern to increase penalties for recidivists. Finally there was the need to modify imprisonment in the light of the new concept of the usefulness of penalties already referred to, which stressed that the stay in prison should be aimed at the social rehabilitation and the moral improvement of the prisoner.

1. With regard to the first of these new ideas about prison, that is its injurious effect (especially in the case of short term loss of liberty), there was a consensus amongst writers, not to say unanimity (because there are always divergent opinions) that it was essential to 'protect first offenders from the pernicious influence of living together. . . .'[1] Ferri took up this idea a little later, declaring: 'As to adult occasional offenders, it is no longer necessary to stress the absurdity and the danger of short-term detention'.[2]

2. Similarly, most lawyers were in agreement on the second reform, which was to make penalties for persistent offenders more severe in an attempt to combat the growth of recidivism. This *phenomenon* was emphasized in reports on the administration of criminal justice. The inadequacy of sentences to check such an increase was referred to as follows: 'It seems that from now on we can affirm that the repressive laws are in themselves powerless to combat recidivism effectively'.[3] This twofold acknowledgement of the increase in recidivism and of the lack of an effective penal solution did not fail to make an impression on the reforming legislators and was to decide the direction of their approach.

It is interesting to note that while the suspended sentence, 'that measure of wise clemency, of intelligent indulgence',[4] came about through a desire to mitigate the punishment of first offenders, it is equally attributable to the opposite desire to strengthen the punishment of persistent offenders.

[1] Desportes and Lefebure, *La science pénitentiaire au Congrès de Stockholm*, Paris, 1880: Cf. similarly Griffiths (Inspector of Prisons) who said at the Geneva Congress in 1897: 'For first offenders prison is useless'. *Proceedings of the Congress*, p. 393.
[2] Ferri, *La sociologie criminelle*, 2nd French edition, 1905, p. 610.
[3] Extract from a report quoted by J. Negre, *La loi Bérenger et ses applications*, Paris, 1892, p. 11.
[4] Definition given by Tarde in 'La loi du sursis conditionnel, et ses effets en France', Saint Petersburg Conference Reports, *Bull. de l'Union intern. de droit pén.*, 1902, p. 296.

3. The third idea which guided the penologists is the most important, since it not only questioned the penalty of loss of liberty in its practical applications, but its very existence and the necessity for it at all. A new conception of punishment was born: from being a means of expiation for the fault committed, punishment had to become an effective instrument for the improvement of the offender, which led logically to the question of *alternative sentences*.

The lawyers were not in agreement on this point. Many of them still thought that 'prison is a necessary evil . . . it is an essential cog in the system of repression'.[1] Similarly certain writers remained cautious in expressing an opinion, for instance Rossi, who wrote: 'In other words, to sacrifice the principle of punishment in the system of social justice, because of exaggerated hopes of reforming the offender, would be to forget the legislator's most essential duties'.[2] But this guarded and pessimistic view was balanced by those of others such as Tarde: 'For the protection of society, the execution of sentences is less important than their pronouncement in court'.[3]

We can detect in this new attitude towards punishment an echo of earlier views, those of Beccaria in particular: 'among all the punishments and the ways of inflicting them, we must choose the one which, proportionately speaking, will make the most effective and lasting impression on the minds of other men, and the least cruel on the criminal'.[4]

But, just as Beccaria's ideas had aroused vehement opposition in the seventeenth century, there was very strong resistance at the end of the nineteenth from the traditional lawyers, particularly when they were confronted with the first proposals concerning suspension.

The question was brought up at two penal and penitentiary congresses, held in Rome in 1885 and St Petersburg in 1890. These congresses studied whether or not certain short-term prison sentences might be avoided and whether it might be

[1] Leveille, *Bull. Soc. gén. prisons*, 1893 (discussion of penalties which might be substituted for imprisonment).
[2] Rossi, *Traité de droit pénal*, 3rd edn., Paris, 1863, Vol. 2, p. 245.
[3] Tarde, 'La loi du sursis conditionnel et ses effets en France', *Bull. de l'Union intern. de dr. pén.*, 1902, p. 301.
[4] Beccaria, *Des délits et des peines*, 6th edn. (French), 1773, para. XII, p. 65.

possible to allow either a simple admonition from the judge or to give him the right to stipulate that the punishment would not be carried out for a minor offence by a first offender. Von Liszt was, of course, very much in favour of this, but von Kirchenheim, professor at Heidelberg, was definitely opposed to the conditional sentence, claiming that it was contrary to the fundamental principles of penal law, that it would lead to arbitrary decisions by the judge and 'overthrow the accepted ideas of morality which are at the basis of society'. Many other participants, and especially certain Russian professors present at the congress, showed the same doubts.[1] Even today this opposition has not completely disappeared among certain Western criminal lawyers; there was an echo of it, for example, in the statements of Professor Messina, at the Bellagio seminar in 1961.

Advocates of the adoption of the suspended sentence—von Liszt in Germany, Garofalo in Italy, Bérenger in France—had a difficult task before them. However, ideas and institutions developed in such a way as to bring about a climate favourable to its adoption. Among the factors involved, we should at least mention the following:

1. In the nineteenth century many legislatures had maintained or, as we have already stated, had restored admonition pronounced by the judge; we find it in several nineteenth-century penal codes, particularly those of certain Italian provinces before the Unification and the Penal Code of 1889. It was proposed as an alternative penalty by several delegates to the Conference in Rome in 1885. Obviously, if it were permissible for the judge simply to 'reprimand' the offender without pronouncing sentence, it had also to be admitted that the judicial determination of an offence did not necessarily entail the pronouncement of a legal punishment.

2. The second half of the nineteenth century saw the appearance and the development of the institution of conditional release. Here again, an important Penitentiary Congress, this time in Stockholm in 1878, stressed the advantages. Gradually continental legislatures had to adopt this institution, first proposed

---

[1] Account of the meeting of the Societé générale des prisons, 16th December 1885. *Bull. Sté. Gén. des Pris.*, 9th year, 1885, p. 786, and *Actes du Congrès pénitentiaire international de Saint-Pétersbourg*, 1890, vol. I, pp. 157–220, vol. II, pp. 475–86 and 487–504.

by the penitentiary school which had developed particularly in France and Belgium between 1830 and 1875, and which had been reinforced on the Continent, by experience drawn this time from the common law countries and the system of tickets of leave.

Conditional release allowed the delinquent whose offence was not too serious and who had shown good conduct during custody to obtain suspension of part of his sentence. Consequently it became apparent that the complete execution of the sentence was not necessarily inevitable, as the traditional penologists had claimed. At the same time, conditional release developed the idea that, by giving the offender a certain advantage, he could in a sense be encouraged to rehabilitate himself. This idea was a new one and had far-reaching developments subsequently, and this is why we have claimed that conditional release was a true forerunner of suspension.[1]

3. We must not forget the influence of the newly emerging penology of the time. After the penitentiary school of Charles Lucas and Ducpétiaux, interest was aroused in the experiments and teachings of Maconochie, Crofton, and later Brockway: gradually it was seen that several categories of convicts existed and that the individual who incurred a punishment should not be considered as an abstract and depersonalized being in the penal institution. The sentence was no longer thought of as a modern version of the ancient practice of branding the criminal with a red-hot iron: it was applied to an individual according to his personal characteristics, assessed biologically, psychologically and anthropologically.

4. So punishment came to be studied, not only from the legal viewpoint as juridical compensation for an offence, but from the social point of view of its practical effectiveness, since one of the essential problems was to prevent recidivism. At the end of the nineteenth century an alarming increase in recidivism led to a questioning of the system of repression which was in force at the time. The father of Senator Bérenger—promoter of the 1891 law—made this statement in a report to the Academy of Moral and Political Sciences in 1853–1854: 'The number of relapses is considerable and over a certain number of years we have seen a great increase . . . we must make a concerted attack . . . and

[1] Cf. J. Nègre, *La loi Bérenger et ses applications*, Paris, 1892, and Desportes and Lefèbure, *La science pénitentiaire au Congrès de Stockholm*, Paris, 1880.

above all we must have recourse to preventive measures'. The very title of Bérenger's Bill—'Bill on the progressive augmentation of sentences in cases of recidivism and on their mitigation for first offences'—shows that this also arose from the desire to ensure an effective fight against recidivism. From then on the traditional idea of repression built up by the classical and neo-classical schools seemed totally inadequate. Almost everyone was agreed in denouncing the detrimental effect of short-term prison sentences, and these were very frequent. In 1889, for example, 48,761 sentences of one to five days in prison were pronounced. The application of extenuating circumstances also entailed the frequent pronouncement of one-month prison sentences. The convicted men were too numerous and stayed too short a time in prison to do any useful work at all. They therefore remained idle and lived in a promiscuity which armed them with all the information necessary to lead a life of crime instead of taking their place once more as law-abiding citizens. Garofalo, at the above-mentioned Congress of Rome, boldly declared that no prison sentence of less than four months should be pronounced.[1] This desire to avoid short sentences was certainly one of the essential bases of the suspended sentence, and Sutherland has rightly stated that whatever the method used to suspend the execution of a sentence, such suspension has been essentially a substitute for imprisonment.

5. We must now consider two lines of thought which, though they started from completely different positions, nevertheless have moved in the same direction. The first of these is, as we have already indicated, the tradition of Beccaria, according to which the best punishment is always the least cruel but the most effective, that is, the one which makes the most lasting impression on the convicted man. Beccaria even put forward—and in this he was before his time—the idea of *prevention*. It was this idea that Bérenger, the father of the suspended sentence, first advocated when light offences do not call for exemplary repression: every effort has then to be made to prevent recidivism. This trend of

---

[1] This idea was taken up, perhaps even more boldly, in Great Britain by the Criminal Justice Act of 1967, which imposed suspension for all sentences of up to six months imprisonment, unless the offence was one of assault, or the offender had had a prison sentence previously or was subject to probation at the time.

ideas, going back to the humanitarianism of the Age of Enlightenment, was augmented by the twentieth-century trend towards the individualization of punishment.

In reaction against the rigidity of classical penal law, it was increasingly hoped that judges would be able to adapt the penal sanction to the character of the offender. This concern guided Senator Bérenger in the drawing-up of his bill, since, as he declared during a Senate debate: 'If a law is to be a good one, if a measure of repression is to produce salutary effects, it is not enough for the punishment laid down to be proportional to the gravity of the offence; it is also necessary, and perhaps most important of all, for it to be in keeping with the moral state of the person on whom it must fall'.[1]

Saleilles, author of a famous work called *L'individualisation de la peine*, published in 1898, stated that the adoption of the suspended sentence was the highest degree of individualization. Bérenger's law was, he said, a law of criminal policy, in contrast with the old penal law which pursued an absolute and merely retributive justice, because Bérenger's law allowed differentiation of punishment according to the individual. Here the actual execution of the penalty is suppressed. Since an offence has been committed a penalty is due. There has to be a punishment, but, Saleilles added, 'society will behave as a creditor does when he forgives a debt, because he has an interest in the individual debtor'.

These various currents of thought gradually accustomed people to the idea of suspended execution of sentence. Admittedly the advocates of reform ran into great resistance; besides those who resolutely opposed the suspended sentence in the name of classical principles, there were those who tried to dismiss the proposed innovation as futile. Would it not be sufficient, they argued, to authorize the judge to pronounce simply an admonition (as did the Italian codes which we have mentioned, or the Portuguese Code of 1852, Art. 42 and 265), thus avoiding this 'judicial suspension' of sentence which so shocked many traditional lawyers.

---

[1] Session of 23rd May 1890 (*J.O. Sénat*, 1890, p. 490). The Minister of Justice expressed the same idea when he addressed the House in these terms: 'It is for the judge to assess, when confronted with an individual who has never been prosecuted, whether or not there is a chance that he will relapse and whether he should be granted provisional liberty'.

Such were the different positions of writers on the problem and the various currents of thought which preceded the putting forward of Bérenger's Bill and the introduction of the suspended sentence in France. As we have seen, these are no more than the early origins of the law of 1891, but they are very real origins, unlike the historical antecedents recalled at the beginning of this chapter.

IMMEDIATE BACKGROUND

Here we must examine in turn the currents of thought which brought about this reform and the parliamentary work which put it into effect.

As we said at the beginning of this chapter, the idea of the suspended sentence was in the air at the time the Bérenger Bill was presented. Thus, Bérenger himself said: 'I don't claim to be an innovator; my proposition has arisen from data collected here and elsewhere, some from abroad; but it has been fortunate enough to meet with a climate of opinion which in a short time has carried it a long way. Belgium has been the first to endorse it, although diminishing the judge's discretion.'[1]

This climate of opinion, which was of paramount importance, expressed itself in two main ways: (1) in legislation, (2) in congresses.

1. If we glance at the legislation of various countries at the time that the law on suspended sentences was passed, we see similar efforts to prevent recidivism and to avoid short-term prison sentences. Thus, the German Penal Code of 1871 (Art. 59) provided for reprimand of minors of 12 to 18 years who were found guilty of knowingly committing a serious offence or misdemeanour. The climate of opinion there, too, was favourable to the idea of conditional sentence, and numerous draft bills were presented to this effect (Wirth, Hippel, Liszt, Aschrott).

In Austria a draft bill put forward in 1889 by the Minister of Justice, Count Schönborn, recommended that the court should be able to suspend the consequences of a conviction for first offenders of fixed abode if the sentence was less than six months in prison.

The Italian Penal Code of 1889 allowed judicial reprimand

[1] *Bull. de la Soc. des prisons*, 1890, p. 724.

(Art. 26 and 27) to be substituted for a sentence not exceeding one month's detention, three months' house arrest or 300 francs fine, providing that it was a first offence and that the offender undertook to pay the agreed fine if he should commit a further, similar offence within a period specified by the judge. The limits of this period were a maximum of two years for serious offences and one year for misdemeanours.

The Portuguese Penal Code of 1886 (Art. 81 and 119) made provision for a reprimand to be pronounced in place of the normal penalty.

Russia also had a special and distinct form of reprimand, applicable to offences committed by civil servants (Art. 65 of the 1845 Code) and, in Article 40 of the Code, reprimand for a certain number of ordinary offences is especially recommended. As far as misdemeanours were concerned, a reprimand was provided for those committed through negligence and without the intention of doing harm. (Art. 9 of the regulation on penalties of one to five days' imprisonment or small fines.)

In Switzerland, in the canton of Appenzell, reprimand was applicable to minors of 12 to 16 years who had knowingly committed minor misdemeanours and in the canton of Vaud it applied to all offenders in the same circumstances.

The most direct source of the suspended sentence was undoubtedly probation. In 1869 the State of Massachusetts legalized the judge's authority to suspend prosecution for a trial period where young delinquents were concerned, and this was extended to adults in 1878 and 1880. We should mention that probation was introduced in New Zealand in 1886—well before it was made law in England.

We should recall, finally, the Belgian law on the suspended sentence, still known as the Lejeune Act, which came into force in 1889, thus preceding the French law.

2. At scientific meetings and conferences, the debating point everywhere was how to combat recidivism effectively, and how to replace prison sentences, particularly short-term imprisonment, by some means which would avoid their detrimental effects, one of which was to pave the way for that recidivism. We need only refer to the congress at Stockholm (1878), to the Fifth International Penitentiary Congress, Paris (1895) to see the bitterness of the debates between those who were fighting for

ORIGINS 15

strict legality and those who wished to rehabilitate convicted men.

Before examining the historical facts surrounding the French law on the suspended sentence, we should say a few words about the Belgian law, which differs from Bérenger's only in certain methods of application (for example, the conditions to be fulfilled before the suspended sentence became effective) but which basically embodies the same purpose and principles. This similarity of views should not come as a surprise, since the Lejeune Act is really only an adaptation of a first draft put forward by Bérenger; the jurists and legislators in Belgium managed to get the bill through parliament before their French colleagues.

The Belgian law of 1888 is, therefore, derived from a French draft bill of 1884, which explains the analogies between the two systems and justifies the term 'Franco-Belgian system'. Bérenger was pleased to recall this fact during the drawing-up of the French law, observing that 'the idea had perhaps appeared a bit daring at the time the first draft was submitted (May 1884). It was, in fact, being put forward for the first time. It has since attracted many important supporters. . . . Finally, the Belgian government . . . submitted to their Parliament a similar bill, whose origins they did not conceal. . . . This bill became law on 31st May, 1888, and is known also as the law on conditional sentence.'[1] The Belgian law, therefore, is of only relative interest for this study and we shall devote few words to it here.

The Belgian law seems to authorize the system of conditional sentence, since the term is employed in the very title of the Act and throughout the legislative text. In reality, it deals, as does the French Act, with the suspension of the execution of a sentence. The discrepancy exists in the text explaining its purposes and aims: sometimes 'suspension of the execution of penalties' and sometimes 'sentence under the suspensive condition of a relapse'. After debates in parliament, the following restatement was made: 'Sentence, conditional or otherwise, is a fact which cannot be erased . . . but it is considered as null and void from the point of view of the penalty entailed. . . .'[2]

Legal writers defined the institution thus: 'conditional sentence

[1] Session of the Senate of 6th March 1890, Bérenger's report (*J.O.*, 1890, *Doc. parlementaires*, Annexe No. 27, p. 68).

[2] *Annales parlementaires*, Senate 1888, p. 438 (quoted by Berger in *Le système de probation anglais et le sursis continental*, Geneva, 1953).

is a penalty which consists of the threat of execution'.[1] Or 'conditional sentence is a true sentence comprising a penalty whose execution is suspended and an admonition which is a moral punishment'.[2]

These, then were the characteristics of the Belgian law of 1888 on conditional sentence which we felt we should mention. Its application must have been encouraging, since the Minister of Justice declared in a report on its administration during the year 1895 that 'the facts do not belie the hopes of the authors of the bill'.[3]

We must now take a brief look at the stages in the fight against recidivism which preceded the adoption of the law on the suspended sentence. In France, the law of 5th June 1875 replaced imprisonment in association by separate imprisonment, and the law of 14th August 1885 authorized conditional release. But these two laws, deceptive in their practical application, were not sufficient to stop the increase in recidivism, hence the necessity for further reform and the need to direct the choice of the legislators toward preventive rather than repressive measures.

This choice of prevention in preference to repression was one of the ideas put forward by Ferri, who considered that 'for occasional offenders social defence should above all be of a preventive rather than a repressive nature'.[4]

The time was ripe for legislative reform. And although such reform was at first so delayed in France that the Bérenger bill went through sooner in Belgium, it was finally achieved in favourable circumstances.

A draft bill was put to the Senate on 26th May 1884. The proposed reform provided for a gradation of penalties and contained two new ideas which were a departure from the general principles of the existing Penal Code. One of these ideas, which does not concern us here, was an augmentation of the punishment in cases of recidivism; but the other was a mitigation of punishment for first offenders. This was the *suspended sentence*, the aim of which was, according to the author of the proposal,

[1] Nypels and Servais, *Traité*, p. 446.
[2] Ch. van H. 'La condamnation conditionelle' in *Rev. dr. pén. et de crim.*, 1939, p. 894.
[3] *Bull. Soc. gén. des prisons*, 1897, p. 1393.
[4] Ferri, *La sociologie criminelle*, 2nd French edn., 1905, p. 609.

'to mitigate the punishment sufficiently to avoid the dangers of imprisonment, while preserving the painful aspect of a penalty, which a simple fine does not generally achieve in our present moral state'.

Among the various sessions during which this proposition was examined, we must mention especially that of 6th March 1890, where Bérenger reported on behalf of the Senate Commission. The following modifications were made in the original draft: the granting of suspension would no longer depend on extenuating circumstances; suspension of sentence would not be applicable to fines, nor to costs, nor to damages, but would cover, unless it was decided to the contrary, accessory penalties and disqualifications resulting from the sentence.

The draft bill was debated in the Senate from 23rd May to 4th July 1890 and was submitted to the Chamber of Deputies at the special session of 1890. The principle of the suspended sentence was unanimously agreed. An amendment by Trarieu, relating to the penalty of the fine, was incorporated: the possibility of suspension was allowed for fines as well. Finally the Commission's text was passed by the Chamber with one modification: the option of suspension should not be applicable to accessory penalties and disqualifications.

On 19th March 1891 the bill, passed by the Chamber, was returned to the Senate; it was submitted, accompanied by a new report by Bérenger, and was followed by renewed debate. The bill was passed by the Senate at the session of 21st March and the law was proclaimed on 26th March 1891.

These, then, were the different stages in the drawing-up and the discussion of Bérenger's bill—the culmination of the penologists' endeavours to bring about a measure which would increase the penalties for habitual offenders who commit minor offences, while at the same time substituting a new penalty for imprisonment as a deterrent against crime.[1]

We do not propose to examine the content of the reports and debates in detail, but it is appropriate to mention the main ideas put forward by Senator Bérenger, through which we can understand the true meaning of the Act and of the institution of the suspended sentence.

[1] Session of the Senate, 6th March 1890, Bérenger's report (*J.O. Doc. Parl.*, Annexe No. 27, p. 68).

The author of the 1891 Act was concerned above all to demonstrate the effectiveness of this judicial warning—doubtless in the hope of reassuring those who still preferred a severe penal sanction and who thought it too 'dangerous' to try this attempted forbearance.[1] Bérenger stated realistically that 'we must beware of falling into the trap of exaggerated philanthropy and, in yielding somewhat to forbearance, we should not lose sight of those guarantees which are indispensable to the safety of society'.[2]

Another of Senator Bérenger's ideas is, we feel, worthy of note. According to him, 'the intention of the proposal is not to establish a distinction between serious and minor offences—the law has provided for that by the flexibility of sentences—but to create a special treatment for the man who has not previously been prosecuted and whose moral character, despite his offence, has remained sufficiently intact for society to have nothing to fear from his liberty'.[3] This consideration of the moral state of the offender replaced the idea of the objective gravity of the offence and, in this respect, it might be said that Bérenger's proposals were situated fairly and squarely in the perspective of modern criminal policy.

Nevertheless there were writers, of whom Ferri was one, who feared that this undoubtedly benevolent measure might have 'neither the true effectiveness nor the frequent application required by the numerous categories of casual offenders committing minor breaches of law'.[4] For the conditional sentence to achieve its desired aim, he continued, it must operate within the framework of a profoundly reformed system of penal justice. Moreover, Ferri deplored the fact that 'the champions of the conditional sentence, for the most part undecided as between the classical theory and that of the positivists, . . . remain somewhere between the two. Admittedly they consider the offender more than the offence, but it is an "average", abstract offender, not a living, breathing being, like those observed in the various anthropological categories.'[5]

Despite the reservations and doubts voiced by this eminent

---

[1] Session of 8th June 1890, M. de l'Angle Beaumanoir's opinion.
[2] Session of 6th March 1890, Bérenger's report already quoted, p. 68.
[3] Report quoted above, p. 69.
[4] Ferri, *La sociologie criminelle*, 1905, 2nd French edn., p. 611.
[5] Ferri, *op. cit.*, p. 616.

Italian author, Senator Bérenger's main ideas can be considered, on the whole, as sound and valid. He was not, in fact, wrong in thinking that this stipulation of good behaviour could effectively protect society and prevent recidivism.

By the same token, although the reform was not devoid of humanitarian aims, and although it did, indisputably, constitute a measure of indulgence towards first offenders, the essential aim of the reformers was not to reduce deterrence, but to ensure the effectiveness of the social reaction to crime. Going back once more to Beccaria, and even Bentham, they considered that what was important was not punishment for punishment's sake but, when possible—and by means of new procedures—to avoid criminal contagion and the offender's return to delinquency. Above and beyond retributive repression, which claims, in moral terms, to be sufficient unto itself, it was essential, on a sociological level, to seek a really effective method of preventing recidivism. Perhaps we can discern in all this a certain socialization of penal law; we can certainly see in it a new recourse to rational application of a modern criminal policy.

II

The Conditional Sentence from the Legal Standpoint

FROM what we have already said, it appears that the suspended sentence is essentially a legal institution, introduced into the legal systems of continental countries at the end of the nineteenth century. To understand exactly what 'the conditional sentence' represents, we must see it first of all from the legal standpoint, and in many respects this analysis is the essence of any general study on the institution of the suspended sentence.

While we do not want to go into all the technical details, we must describe the way in which the conditional sentence has been adjusted so as to fit into the general system of penal law on the continent. To do this thoroughly, we must first describe the basic principles of the institution, then examine the circumstances in which conditional sentences can be pronounced, and finally discuss their effects. We shall then be able to draw several general conclusions, by way of completing this study.

THE BASIC PRINCIPLES OF THE INSTITUTION

It must be understood that the adoption of the suspended sentence was a considerable innovation in the legal systems of continental countries at the end of the nineteenth century. It was contrary to retributive legal principles, such as those that had guided the classical penal law established in continental Europe since the end of the eighteenth century, under the influence of Montesquieu, Beccaria, Bentham and Feuerbach. Under that system, only the law could fix the penalties; the judge pronounced them when he recognized the existence of the offence, but he had logically no choice at all in the determination of penalties. The fixing of penalties was the prerogative of the law and in the beginning it was even declared that the judge could not explain the legal provisions which defined punishable offences. Furthermore, once the legal penalty was pronounced, nothing could save the offender from its application.

Perhaps the most complete expression of this system was the French Penal Code of 1791, revised in the light of the Declaration of the Rights of Man and the Citizen of 1789. The law laid down fixed penalties for crimes and the exact amount of these penalties was prescribed in a text that was binding on everyone. This penal code abolished the pre-Revolutionary 'Letters of favour and remission' by which the king could absolve a convicted person from the execution of his sentence. For the philosophers of 1789 the law applied even to the sovereign, and nobody could suspend a legally incurred and properly pronounced sentence.

Penal science, particularly the Italo-German school, which developed in the nineteenth century, had added a kind of equation to this concept of criminal policy: crime = punishment. Punishment thus seemed to be the necessary juridical consequence of an offence. Its essential function was seen as the restoration of law and order, which had been destroyed or threatened by the crime. The means of doing this was the effective infliction of a sanction, which also had to be of an essentially juridical nature. In the Hegelian dialectic, it was considered that since crime was the negation of law and order, the punishment for it should negate the crime itself, in such a way that the negation of the negation would suppress the very existence of the offence. As the offence was a 'juridical entity', according to Carrara's definition, punishment itself was a legal concept on which considerations of fact and the individual circumstances of the offender should have no bearing.

Such a system was obviously fundamentally hostile to all ideas of a conditional sentence. The classical jurists of 1791 or of 1810, the date of the Napoleonic Penal Code, could not have conceived it. In the nineteenth century the neo-classical school mitigated to a certain extent the harshness of the law on this point. The right of pardon was quickly restored and judges were allowed a certain discretion in penalties between fixed maxima and minima. In 1832 a flexible system of extenuating circumstances was even established in France. If the judge thought that there were 'extenuating circumstances', he could go below the legal minimum set down by the law. Nevertheless, the neo-classical jurists of the mid-nineteenth century refused in principle to admit that the judge could decide whether or not the sentence which he pronounced should be carried out. Carrara considered that such a possibility would be contrary to the judge's judicial role, which according to him consisted simply in pronouncing the sentence when he had established the existence of the offence beyond any doubt. It was argued that it would constitute an infringement of the power of pardon, which belonged to the sovereign, or that of conditional release, which was an administrative matter.

It was in such a climate of opinion that the first moves to bring in the suspended sentence met with strong resistance. We felt it necessary to mention all these factors in studying the direct sources of the Franco-Belgian reform of 1889–1891. It must be remembered that these controversies, these currents of thought and the very climate of opinion in which the legislative changes were proposed, explain the nature, the character and the conditions of the reform. In fact, because of what preceded it, the reform could be accepted on the continent only insofar as it was presented as a limited exception to the traditional rules of penal law, and above all if it could avoid conflict with those fundamental principles which continental jurists and legislators still hold dear. The suspended sentence, if accepted, should not upset the traditional functioning of penal justice.

This accounts for the basic positions which the reformers adopted and which must be kept in mind if we are to understand the true significance of conditional sentence. First of all, this would have to constitute a *special legal institution*, having its own particular characteristics, having its scope regulated by law, and being capable of a theoretical, and even dogmatic interpretation true to the neo-classical doctrine. This point has sometimes been lost sight of, but it seems to us essential to a true understanding of the suspended sentence. Similarly, and at the same period, Carl Stoos (author of the famous Swiss draft penal code of 1894, which had considerable repercussions upon the legal systems of the continent and Latin America), when he wanted to bring in non-punitive measures to secure the treatment of mentally abnormal offenders, or measures of restraint for habitual recidivists, had to present the new measures he advocated in the form of legally constructed judicial institutions. This is why, in order to stress in legal terminology that they were different from traditional penalties, he called them 'preventive measures'. Similarly, the promoters of the suspended sentence were obliged to devote themselves to an autonomous legal construction.

In the second place, the positions adopted by the promoters of the suspended sentence—or the positions which were thrust upon them—meant that they had to rule out any idea of suspending the *imposition* of sentence. The traditional system, entrenched for a hundred years by the time the idea of the suspended sentence appeared, was necessarily opposed to any suggestion that the establishment of the existence of an offence should not be followed immediately by sentence to a punishment laid down by the law. It was thought that the whole concept of a penal justice subject to the rule of law would be tainted if a judge were allowed either to declare an individual guilty without inflicting a punishment or to choose not to pronounce a sentence on the accused brought before him by law.

Finally, and for the same reasons, the promoters of the suspended sentence, Bérenger in France and Lejeune in Belgium, had to put aside any idea of assistance to, or supervision of, the offender who was granted conditional suspension of punishment. The aim of the conditional sentence was essentially to intimidate the casual offender, not yet completely involved in a life of crime.[1] In 1888 Lejeune declared before the Belgian parliament that those for whom suspension was envisaged had no need of assistance because they 'would rehabilitate themselves'. For

[1] The principle of the conditional sentence, as we have already mentioned, has met with lively doctrinal resistance. Take the three main elements of opposition. First of all the principles of the neo-classic retributive school of thought have been confirmed anew at the Bellagio Seminar (29th April–1st May 1961) in Professor Messina's speeches. Then, too, the existence of related institutions, such as admonition, or judicial reprimand, which are accepted as satisfactory (Sardinian/Neapolitan Code, Tuscan Code and Portuguese Penal Code of 1852, Art. 42 and 265) are a tremendous obstacle to the acceptance of the suspended sentence.

Finally, we must take account of administrative measures of clemency or favour; it is by this means that conditional release was admitted by certain of those who reject the suspended sentence on doctrinal grounds (like Carrara). They found the former institution preferable because it entailed a 'taste' of imprisonment (supposed to be exemplary and retributive) and it rewarded good conduct following the offence and under restraint. In the German system it was pardon which stood in the way of the suspended sentence.

S.S.—2

related, but different reasons, they also put aside any idea of the supervision of the offender whose sentence was suspended.

This was a time, in fact, when there was a total lack of social workers in the judicial sphere; the only supervision which could have been arranged therefore, would have been by the police. Now 'police supervision', which had been introduced for many convicted men by the Penal Code of 1810, had just been abolished in France in 1885. Its evils had been boldly denounced by Victor Hugo in *Les Misérables*, it had left bad memories behind it and was largely repudiated by liberal penal law. So, what was it all about? Simply a matter of establishing the existence of an offence, not sending the offender to serve a short-term prison sentence, but offering him the chance to rehabilitate himself through good behaviour. In pronouncing the conditional sentence, the judge would explain to the offender the favour which he was being granted and warn him of the danger to which he would expose himself if he committed a further offence. This favour, accompanied by a precise and, in a sense, calculated threat, was the salient feature of the suspended sentence in the minds of its promoters and of those who accepted it. It is the fundamental basis of the new institution.

From this was to grow the particular Franco-Belgian technique of the suspended sentence, with its own features, and its strict judicial formulations, but also its possibilities of development. For we see more clearly today than did the contemporaries of Bérenger and Lejeune, that the suspended sentence was not, as Saleilles thought, the end of an evolution. It was, on the contrary, a point of departure towards new developments.

To start with, however, the institution was fragile and it will remain so for a long time. It is threatened mainly by those who persist in seeing it as an encouragement to crime, who claim that it makes the first step on the road to crime painless. It will be threatened also by the authoritarian tendencies which became apparent in various penal legislatures during the first half of the twentieth century, advocating the relentless reinforcement of immediately executed punishments. Finally, another threat to the stability of the suspended sentence can be that uncontrollable factor, public opinion and its panic reaction to certain types of offence. There are times when, in certain countries the option of granting conditional sentence is abolished or suspended. This is what the Vichy government did in France for numerous offences. On 11th February 1951, a law had to be passed to give judges back the power freely to grant a suspended sentence or take account of extenuating circumstances.

The Egyptian Code of 1904, amended in 1925, 1937 and 1953, also excludes the possibility of granting a suspended sentence for certain offences (otherwise totally dissimilar), which range from drug peddling to misdemeanours concerned with catering. A Polish law of 22nd May 1958 rules out the suspended sentence for offences involving 'hooliganism'. In the most recent legislation of Senegal, suspended sentence for embezzlement depends on the reimbursement of the amount embezzled. These are only a few examples, but they suffice to show what problems have been posed, in the legal systems of the continental civil-law countries, by the introduction, the development, and even the continuance of the suspended sentence.

CONDITIONS FOR GRANTING A SUSPENDED SENTENCE

To give an exact picture of the legal mechanism of the conditional sentence, we feel we must go back to the Franco-Belgian technique. We shall lay particular emphasis on the conditions under which suspension can be granted, because they form the legal framework of the institution.

Obviously these conditions vary according to the country and its legal system. They were not even identical in France and Belgium, in the original statutory forms of the conditional sentence. On the other hand, it is easy to understand that when the institution spread to other countries, it became diversified and acquired new shades of meaning. This is why in a later chapter we shall explain more precisely the various laws governing the suspended sentence in different countries. Such comparison is not the purpose of this present chapter, however, because we feel that we should explain the significance and the essence of the institution in relation to its actual application, before pointing out the differences between the legal systems which recognize it. Here, therefore, we are looking mainly at the Franco-Belgian system in its fundamental unity, concentrating upon the common rules which it sought to establish.

The conditions relate to the kind of penalties which can be suspended, the offenders who can benefit and the methods or procedure to be followed by judges in granting a suspended sentence.

Which Penalties can be Suspended?

All that we have said previously has already indicated that the suspended sentence can be granted only for relatively unimportant penalties. France and Belgium have a traditional tripartite division, which distinguishes between criminal penalties, resulting from the most serious offences and pronounced by the Assizes; correctional penalties for lesser offences pronounced by the ordinary *tribunaux correctionnels*; and finally penalties called '*de simple police*', pronounced in a lower court by a justice of the peace and applying to the least serious type of offences, called contraventions. These last have for a long time been dealt with only by very small fines; so that it was pointless to provide that they should qualify for suspended sentences, the object of which was to stop first offenders coming into contact with prison life. In its basic conception, therefore, the conditional sentence was advocated essentially for correctional penalties, which are, traditionally, up to five years' imprisonment or a fine. Obviously, on this basis, there was no question of applying the suspended sentence to solitary confinement, hard labour, or, of course, capital punishment.

The Belgian law of 1888 was more restrictive than the French one of 1891, because it permitted suspension only for sentences of six months or less, while the French law referred simply to prison sentences and fines in general. Certain countries were more impressed by the Belgian restrictions than by the French liberality, while yet others excluded suspension of fines.

Bérenger justified the French approach by stating that the aim of the measure was mainly to establish 'special treatment for the man who has not been previously prosecuted and whose moral character, despite his offence, has remained sufficiently intact for society to have nothing to fear from his liberty'.[1] Therefore, judgement must not be based on the 'seriousness of the offence,

[1] Bérenger's report, Senate, 6th March 1890 (*J.O.* 1890, *Doc. Parl.*, Annexe No. 27, p. 69).

but must assess the moral state of the offender and decide how good a guarantee that state offers'.[1] Thus, the main factor to be considered is not the offence committed, but the sentence pronounced for that offence. Under this system it could happen that even a crime (in the technical French sense, that is, an offence normally punished by hard labour or solitary confinement) might result in a conditional sentence if, as a result of the admission of extenuating circumstances, the judge were to reduce the legal sentence by one or two degrees, passing thus from, say, solitary confinement, to imprisonment for less than five years. It makes little difference, either, whether it is a matter of an 'offence in common law' or a political offence: if the sentence pronounced is imprisonment, it can be suspended.

WHICH OFFENDERS CAN BENEFIT FROM THE CONDITIONAL SENTENCE?

The suspended sentence was invented, or constructed, essentially for the *first offender*, that is the man who has never been legally convicted, and who consequently has not come into contact with prison. The first article of the French law of 1891 stated that the suspended sentence can be granted to a man with no previous sentence of imprisonment for crime or for an 'ordinary offence'. It may be observed here that if a political offence qualifies for a conditional sentence, a previous sentence for such an offence would not preclude the granting of a further suspended sentence for an 'offence in common law'. We can detect in this dispensation the old liberal nineteenth-century principle by which a conviction for a political offence has no stigma attached to it. Moreover, in the French system regarding political offences, drawn up from 1832 to 1848, the individual found guilty of such an offence was not, as a rule, sentenced to imprisonment. In fact a special scale of political penalties existed which did not include the death penalty, forced labour, solitary confinement or even imprisonment.

We find the same principle in the Belgian law of 1888, Article 9, of which states that suspension can be granted to a person with no previous sentence for a crime or an offence. Here again, the French law was broader than the Belgian one, because in the latter even a previous sentence of a fine would preclude the

[1] Report quoted above.

granting of a suspended sentence. In Belgium it was even considered that a previous conditional sentence, not followed by recidivism during the legal 'operational period', should stand in the way of a further suspended sentence.[1]

As a consequence of this system, the suspended sentence is designed in line with the traditional view of recidivism. What really constitutes the obstacle to the granting of suspension is not, strictly speaking, a previous *offence*, but a previous *sentence*. Thus it would be possible for a suspended sentence to be granted to offenders who were not, in criminological terms, first offenders, but who were nevertheless individuals who had as yet had no contact with prison.

THE PROCEDURE AND METHODS BY WHICH JUDGES MAY GRANT A SUSPENDED SENTENCE

The main principle here is the *discretionary* nature of suspension: in the original Franco-Belgian system, it never constitutes a right of the offender, and the judge is never obliged to grant it. Those who promoted the reform hoped that the judge would take up the task of individualization, by selecting the offenders who were able to benefit from the favour of conditional liberty. Bérenger and Lejeune both agreed that the judge should be given the widest possible latitude.[2]

Moreover, in the continental civil-law systems which have adopted the conditional sentence, a twofold fear has sometimes been felt. First of all, to simplify his task, the judge may be tempted to grant a suspended sentence automatically to all who qualify for it, thus sacrificing the individualization that had been hoped for. There is also a fear, in the opposite direction, that certain judges may make arbitrary decisions, sometimes granting and sometimes refusing suspension under almost identical circumstances. To avoid these two extremes, certain statutes have sought to provide the criminal judge with some guiding rules concerning the granting of suspended sentences.

[1] See Declaration of Minister Lejeune in the Chamber of Representatives session of 16th May 1888, quoted by Locard, *Commentaire de la loi du 26 mars 1891*, Paris, p. 27.

[2] Bérenger stated in the Senate: 'We must refer the matter to the judge's conscience, which is better able to make the necessary distinctions than is the law'. Session of 9th June 1890 (*J.O.*, 1890, p. 358).

Without giving the details of all these, it would be valuable to mention a few here. The Argentinian Penal Code of 1922, Article 26, laid down that a judge must examine the character of the offender, and even recommended that he should be able, in this respect, to ask for all relevant information to be collected. The Chilean Penal Code of 1906 (Art. 564) required the offender to have had a 'favourable record' and the Swiss code of 1937 (Art. 41) recommended that suspension should be granted only if the record and character of the convicted man were such that this measure would deter him from further offences. The Austrian law of 1952 advocated the conditional suspension of a penalty when the threat of its execution would appear to be more effective than the actual execution itself.

Some special laws went further than these general formulae. Article 88 of the Portuguese Penal Code stated that the degree of guilt and the moral conduct of the offender must be considered as well as the circumstances of the offence. In Spain (Art. 92 *et seq.* of the Penal Code) account had to be taken of age, background, the juridical nature of the act and its circumstances. In Egypt, the law of 1904 (Art. 55) related to the character, the past history and the age of the offender, as well as to the circumstances of the offence, adding that all these factors can help a judge to decide whether a man will abstain from crime in the future. The Italian code of 1930 went even further in this direction by demanding an actual diagnosis of 'non-dangerousness' before granting a suspended sentence.

The possibility of arbitrary decisions on the part of judges is further limited by requiring a special statement of the reasons for granting a suspended sentence.[1] This requirement is very general in the civil-law countries, where, in principle, every judicial decision should be accompanied by reasons. But here again, it may be feared that the judge may be content to use well-established and stereotyped formulae for every conditional sentence. This is why, for example, the Courts of Appeal in

---

[1] In his report to the Senate of 6th March 1890, Bérenger stated that 'subject to certain conditions the judge could be allowed greater powers of indulgence', and he specified in particular that 'execution of a sentence of imprisonment could be suspended by a *decision for which special reasons were given*'. Bérenger's report already quoted (*J.O.*, 1890, *Doc. Parl.*, Annexe No. 27, p. 68).

various Swiss cantons (notably Geneva) and the Federal Court require the special grounds for each particular case. Consequently, in order to justify the refusal of suspension, it would not be sufficient simply to state that the granting of this favour would fail to deter the man from crime, or that his character appeared to rule against it. Nor could the judge, in order to grant suspension, refer in general terms to the character or the moral sense of the offender. It seems that he is required to specify and explain in detail the facts and circumstances which had led to his decision.

Finally, under the original system of suspended sentence, the judge has an important supplementary obligation: he must explain to the convicted man that a penalty has been assigned to him but that the execution of that penalty is suspended on condition that he behaves well and does not commit a further offence during the operational period.[1] The authors of the law stressed the deterrent effect of the threat hanging over the offender, which, in some respects, appeared to them to be the essence of the suspended sentence.[2] The offender is not sent to prison, but is given clearly to understand that he will go there if he relapses into delinquency.[3]

Through the existence and operation of these various legal conditions, we come to understand more exactly the nature of the conditional sentence in the Franco-Belgian system and those derived from it. All these legal features derive, in fact, from the one fundamental idea that the sentence *is* imposed, and only its execution is suspended.

Sentence *is* imposed—this is where we get away from the usual technique of probation, which normally entails postponement of

---

[1] Bérenger justified the necessity for this solemn warning with these words: 'This timely warning would have the double effect of cautioning the convicted man against a relapse into crime and of letting the public know the conditions on which the suspension depends. (Senate session of 6th March 1890, Bérenger's report already quoted, *J.O.*, 1890, *Doc. Parl.*, Annexe No. 27, p. 69).

[2] Prins wrote: 'Who would dare to deny that for novices in crime, the threat is more effective than the penalty?' (quoted by Perrin in *De la remise conditionnelle des peines*, Geneva, 1904, note 2, p. 135). Boitard, for his part, saw this 'judicial warning . . . as an actual punishment, resulting from the prosecution, which might be sufficient where the disturbance of law and order has not been too great.' (*Leçons de droit criminel*, Paris, 1896, No. 883.)

[3] It is interesting to note that the idea of admonition crops up again here.

the imposition of sentence.[1] It is claimed that the actual imposition of sentence is more effective in general prevention and in deterrence. From the point of view of special prevention, the imposed sentence is, as we have just seen, a precise threat which must, as such, have more effect on the convicted man.

Besides, this actual imposition is in line, as we have already pointed out, with the general principles of continental penal law. It pays homage to the legal definition of offences and penalties and the rule according to which the judge's intervention depends upon the established fact that an offence has been committed. In the perspective of classical or neo-classical philosophy, imposition of the penalty is an unavoidable necessity, since punishment is the necessary consequence of the offence and punishment alone can restore the law and order destroyed or compromised by that offence. Finally, from the utilitarian point of view, we would add that, when a sentence is imposed, there remains a record of the offence and of the punishment, without which the proof of the offence might vanish. If a further offence is committed, this record is such as to make it possible to bring into play immediately the principles relating to recidivism to deal with the new offence.

It follows from this concept that the sentence exists. It will thus be written into the court records[2] and more often than not will carry all its other effects except the actual imprisonment of the convicted man (we shall return to this point later).

For the same reasons, and in the same neo-classical perspective, the judge's intervention has been limited as far as possible, apart from his power of individualization, which consists in granting or refusing a suspended sentence. The Franco-Belgian system did not originally advocate any preliminary investigation of personality and the operational period

---

[1] Bérenger thought the English system somewhat dangerous, because he wondered whether 'this retrospective judgement would afford adequate guarantees?' (Bérenger's report, *op. cit.*, p. 68).

[2] During the debates on Bérenger's bill, a proposal was made that conditional sentences should not figure in the court records. The commission rejected this proposal, and Bérenger explains the grounds for their rejection: 'This would deprive the law of an essential piece of information in the case of relapse. And since a third party is always free to ask to see the court records, it would constitute a kind of legal deception, of which the law cannot be guilty'. (Senate, 6th March 1890, report quoted above, *op. cit.*, p. 69.)

in this system was strictly fixed by law. Subsequent laws in various countries have recommended that the fixing of this period should to some extent be left to the judge's discretion. Bérenger maintained that it was not fitting for the judge himself to determine the period during which, in order to be rehabilitated, a man must not commit a further offence.[1] This reasoning, however, occurred in an age when neither investigations nor files on personality were known. Above all, Bérenger's thinking was in the traditional classical perspective, which attempted to guard against an arbitrary decision on the part of the judge. The operational period, in such a conception, could only be fixed by the law and in such a way that it applied to all who benefited from the conditional sentence.

Bérenger was at pains to specify that this period of suspension would be that of the punishment prescribed. After five years, in fact, the convicted man would no longer be liable to undergo the sentence, since the sanction would have been raised. That is the system which became the conditional sentence and this demonstrates again that, in its original conception, this particular measure adhered firmly to the general principles of classical penal law on the Continent. This will become even more apparent, perhaps, when we study the effects of the conditional sentence.

THE EFFECTS OF THE CONDITIONAL SENTENCE

Like the conditions for granting a conditional sentence, its effects are strictly determined by law. But they all derive from the same fundamental principle, that there must definitely be a *conditional sentence*. Legally this means that the sentence exists, but that the execution of the main penalty is suspended on condition that the offender does not commit a further offence. It is these two points that we must now examine.

First of all, *the sentence has been pronounced*. Consequently, a

---

[1] Bérenger justified his ideas as follows: 'Why this uniformity? Because it is a question of undergoing a test, and the conditions of this test must be the same in all cases. Our purpose is not to seek a punishment that is the equivalent of the sentence imposed . . . but to determine the length of time necessary for the offender to show proof positive of his honesty.' (Bérenger, Session of 18th June 1890. *Bull. Soc. gen. des prisons*, 1890, p. 730.)

CONDITIONAL SENTENCE FROM LEGAL STANDPOINT 33

sentence is fixed by the judge and the offence incurs the legal penalty. Just after the law of 1891 was passed, Boitard, a noted penologist of the time, stressed this point both to justify and to explain the law: the guilty man would not go unpunished, he said, but on the contrary, his guilt would be recognized and dealt with.[1] The conditional sentence thus constitutes a penalty, while the more important element in it, the execution of the main penalty, is conditionally suspended. Another well-known French criminal lawyer, Joseph Magnol, was to say the same thing later at the Penal and Penitentiary Congress held in London in 1925: 'the conditional sentence is, for the genuinely casual offender, a solemn and sufficient affirmation of society's disapproval of the offence he has committed'.[2]

Precise judicial consequences follow the imposition of a sentence. If the man who has been conditionally sentenced commits a further infraction, he will find himself in the category of 'recidivists', since he has already been sentenced. Moreover, the fact that he has had a previous sentence will lessen his chances of obtaining a second suspension for a later offence. On the other hand, once sentence has been pronounced and guilt recognized, the convicted man will be able, subject to the normal conditions, to ask for a retrial if new evidence might establish his innocence. He will also be able to ask for, and even obtain, 'reinstatement under ordinary law' if he fulfils the necessary conditions. Finally, once the main sentence has been imposed, all the complementary and accessory penalties will normally come into effect.[3] The sentence will carry with it all its usual civil consequences, particularly insofar as compensation for the victim is concerned.

All these consequences derived from the law and the judge

---

[1] This author wrote: 'The idea of possible suspension of the execution of sentence for relatively minor offences . . . will not result, as has been claimed, in a scandalous failure to punish the guilty man'. (Boitard, *op. cit.*, No. 883.)

[2] Report by Magnol, Congress of London: *Proceedings of the Congress*, Vol. II, p. 170.

[3] It is interesting to know the views of the promoters of the 1891 law on this point: Bérenger summed them up in these terms: 'The Commission felt that these accessory penalties and disqualifications being a direct consequence of the penalty itself, should be suspended with it, at least when the court does not decide otherwise'. (Bérenger's report, already quoted, *op. cit.*, p. 69.)

could not, under the original system of the suspended sentence, put any obstacle in their way. He could, of course, suspend the execution of the main penalty, but he could not, for example, order partial execution of that penalty. Furthermore, he could not, under this system, and indeed according to the philosophy of the suspended sentence, add further effects to the legal ones. In particular, he could not give instructions or orders to the man whose sentence was suspended, nor could he hold him to any special obligation. The only obligation imposed upon the beneficiary of suspension was not to commit a further offence during a given time.

The strictness of this original conception of the suspended sentence has since been tempered. Just as some laws have provided that the judge should fix the length of the operational period between certain legal limits, others have stated that accessory or complementary penalties need not necessarily be applied where the sentence is suspended. In Yugoslavia, for instance, the judge makes an investigation in order to decide whether a ban on practising certain professions or activities should be enforced in a case where the sentence is suspended.

We are presented here with two different concepts. According to the first of these, only the actual execution of imprisonment is suspended. At most, suspension of fines may also be allowed. But all the other effects of the sentence are brought into force, because it is held desirable that the man who has received a suspended sentence should actually be sentenced, and should feel himself to be sentenced.

Another, more recent, conception is that, in principle, none of the consequences of the sentence should take effect in cases where the sentence is conditionally suspended; everything should be held in reserve in case of a further offence. Since the offender is only sentenced subject to a condition, which is the commission of another offence, all the consequences of the sentence are suspended until that condition is fulfilled. The idea of a fresh start and another chance for the convicted man is substituted here for the old notion of the sword of Damocles. Confidence has replaced intimidation and encouragement has replaced the restriction of rights. Here we are approaching, if not the actual technique, at least the climate of probation. However, this was not the original—one might almost say the *pure* concept of the suspended sentence in the minds of the authors of the reform, Bérenger and Lejeune.[1]

The sentence is imposed and exists as such, but the execution, at least of the main penalty, is suspended. That is the essential effect and purpose of the suspended sentence. But we should note that this end is achieved, in the Franco-Belgian system, by the use of the Roman law technique of the *condition*.

The traditional definition of a condition is a future and uncertain element on which depends either the execution or the resolution of a judicial act. If the condition is suspensive, the act has no effect before the condition is fulfilled. If the condition is resolutory, the act will produce all its effects, but the fulfilment of the condition will erase all the consequences, which would then retrospectively disappear.

We have seen that certain writers, soon after the law came into force, talked of the suspensive condition. Perhaps in the original perspective of the Franco-Belgian laws of 1888 and 1891, they should have spoken of the resolutory condition. The sentence existed and produced all its effects, although the main penalty was not carried out; if the convicted man came to the end of the operational period without committing a further offence, then the condition was fulfilled and the sentence was thus retrospectively erased by the operation of civil-law principles.

In the second conception of the suspended sentence, to which we referred just now, we find what is logically a suspensive condition. The sentence is imposed but neither the principal penalty nor the accessory penalties are executed; at the very most the offender is obliged to make reparation for damage caused, but this is a question of a civil obligation and not a penal rule. The condition here, then, is the commission of a further offence, and if it occurs the sentence is then carried out, together with all its provisions.

In any event, we are dealing with a condition in the Roman-law sense of the word, which operates retroactively. From this it follows that:

1. If a further offence is committed, the revocation of the

[1] The author of the 1891 law, set great store by this power of intimidation. He held that the suspended sentence would constitute an ideal system: the minimum of punishment producing the maximum of deterrence. (Report already quoted, *op. cit.*, p. 68.)

suspension takes place in law and in virtue of the law. The occurrence which leads to revocation cannot therefore be anything but the fact that the offender has committed an infraction specified and sanctioned by penal law. It is not a question of bad behaviour or of what is called, in a system of supervised freedom, an 'incident'; only a legally defined offence can bring the offender back before the penal judge.

2. Revocation operates automatically; the judge has simply to pronounce it, without having recourse to other measures, and he is unable to modify the conditions of suspension to fit the new circumstances. Here again is a departure from the idea and the technique of probation.

3. If the conditions are not fulfilled, the sentence is held to be null and void. It is erased retrospectively and the offender is legally reinstated. This reinstatement occurs in law and in virtue of the law; there is no need for the offender to appear before a judge again, and the judge does not have to make any pronouncement or to reappraise his conduct or his status.

Having examined the conditions and the effects of the conditional sentence, we would repeat—to sum up on this point—that it has been built up on the Franco-Belgian system as a strict legal measure, with its application and its consequences clearly defined. In terms of penal policy, however (for it has been said, rightly, that the suspended sentence is a measure of penal policy), it is an institution which, quite apart from its primary object of preventing contact with prison, serves as an instrument of individualization.

It is a favour, or rather a benefit, which the offender can receive from the judge who assesses his personal qualities as well as the circumstances of the offence. But in its original conception it was seen as a solemn warning together with a precise and calculated threat; it was designed for the casual offender not yet corrupted by imprisonment, for the individual whose behaviour and character might be considered normal and in whom, it seems, confidence can be placed on the strength of that warning and that threat.

Consequently, the main essentials are found in the psychological shock of appearing in court, in the offender's realization that he is accountable to the judge, who represents society, and in the period of time during which he must learn to take his place once more as a law-abiding citizen. Here again, the judicial technique of the suspended sentence is based on an idea of penal philosophy. It is wrong to think that under this system the offender is rashly left to his own devices. The idea behind the institution is that he should confront his future alone, with the vivid memory of the sanction pronounced on his past offence and the feeling of the threat which hangs over him should he return to crime. The essence of the Franco-Belgian system of the suspended sentence is founded upon the basic concepts of continental penal law in its traditional and liberal expression. Society may legally punish and, in less serious cases, may be content to reprimand or warn; but it must respect the individual's freedom of behaviour and not invade his personality. The man for whom the ordinary suspended sentence was conceived was that 'rational man who is master of himself' in the Declaration of Rights, 1789, and the free contractant of the Napoleonic Code, 1804.

III

The Geographical Spread of the Suspended Sentence

THE adoption of the suspended sentence by Belgium and France marked a decisive step forward in the history of penal law, and had repercussions throughout the world—in Europe as well as in Latin America, and in the Near East as well as the Far East. Today it is incorporated in the legal systems of certain independent African countries, for example, the Penal Code of the Cameroons.

In the years immediately following the introduction of the Lejeune law and the Bérenger law, the countries which adopted the suspended sentence were usually directly inspired by the Franco-Belgian system and took it over with only slight modifications. After the second world war, countries which had already established the suspended sentence complemented it, in many cases, with measures deriving from probation. And countries which had not yet adopted it generally introduced the ordinary suspended sentence and suspended sentence with *mise à l'épreuve* both at the same time.

Geographically, the development of the suspended sentence was rather sporadic. It would take root in one country, and spread out to its neighbours, sometimes settling into its original form, sometimes evolving new methods and modifications.

HISTORICAL BACKGROUND

In Europe the first countries to adopt the suspended sentence under the direct influence of the French/Belgian reform were Luxembourg, by the law of 10th May 1892, often called by the name of its author, Minister of State Eyschen; then in 1893 Portugal, which introduced conditional sentence and conditional release from prison at the same time in the law of 6th July 1893.

Of the Scandinavian countries, it was Norway that headed the movement and that, by the law of 2nd May 1894, integrated the suspended sentence into its legal system. In 1905 Denmark introduced a similar bill, but instead of adhering simply to the Franco-Belgian system, it was also inspired by the Anglo-Saxon system of probation and was the first continental country to introduce a mixed system. In 1906, the following year, Sweden in its turn adopted the suspended sentence but did not include mention, as Denmark had, of the idea of 'moral treatment'.

Similarly, it was the ordinary suspended sentence that was introduced in Italy by the law of 26th June 1904, sometimes called the Ronchetti Act. It was applied in Bulgaria the same year. Spain and Hungary adopted it in 1908, Greece in 1911 and Finland in 1918.

The Netherlands formulated a régime of suspension (law of 12th June 1915) which, by its results, was to put them in the front line of reform in this field.

In Germany, where the conditional sentence had found an ardent supporter in Liszt, the institution evolved through various phases. Encouraged by the French and Belgian movements, some German states—Saxony and Prussia—modified their legislation in 1895. But they were content at that time to adopt a system in which suspension was still subordinate to pardon, which was an administrative measure. After 1919 this right of conditional pardon passed from the administrative authorities into the hands of the courts in the majority of states. Nevertheless, the judge continued to make his decision only as a delegate of the administrative authorities.

Political vicissitudes had their effect in this field also. The order of 6th February 1935, which applied to the whole territory of the Third Reich, took back this right from the judiciary. In 1945 its regulation was entrusted to the *Länder* governments. It was only with a third statute of 4th August 1953, modifying the penal law, and with the statute concerning juvenile courts of the same date, that the ordinary suspended sentence, or the suspended sentence combined with a probationary régime, was at last regulated for the whole of the Federal German Republic by one text.

The suspended sentence also cropped up in Northern Ireland as the 'recorded sentence', no doubt during the first ten years of the twentieth century, but we cannot ascertain the exact date of its introduction into Irish judicial practice.[1] The sentence meted out to the offender was entered in the records, but he was allowed to go free on condition that he undertook to be of good behaviour and keep the peace during a period laid down by the court.[2]

It was mainly after the first world war that the principle of the suspended sentence reached the east European countries. It appeared in the Leading Principles of the Russian Socialist Federated Soviet Republic of 1919, and the first criminal Code of the RSFSR, of 1922, contains detailed regulations for the conditional sentence. The suspended sentence was introduced in Czechoslovakia in 1919; into Rumanian penal law in 1928; and we find it in the Polish Penal Code of 1932. The fact that these last three countries have become people's democracies has made no difference to the institution of the suspended sentence.

The spread of the suspended sentence has not been limited to Europe, however. In the Far East, Japan drew up a law in 1905 which was modelled on the Franco-Belgian system, and incorporated it in the penal code of 1907, still in force today. In the Near East, Egypt adopted this institution in 1904. In Israel, contrary to the procedure in most other countries, the suspended sentence, introduced in 1954, was grafted on to the system of probation which was already in existence.[3] In Turkey the first rule regarding suspension was inserted in the Penal Code of 1926.

Of the Latin American countries, it was Chile which first instituted the ordinary suspended sentence in 1906, then followed in quick succession Argentina, Brazil, Costa Rica, Colombia, Cuba, Ecuador, Guatemala, Mexico, Panama, Peru and Uruguay. On the other hand, Salvador has only lately come round to the idea of the conditional sentence, and in 1957 opted for suspension with *mise à l'épreuve*.

In Africa the Cameroons voted in 1965 for a Penal Code, applied since 1966, which recommended both the ordinary suspended sentence and suspension with probation.[4]

---

[1] Cf. Nial Osborough 'The Suspended Sentence in Northern Ireland', in *The Irish Jurist*, vol. II, New Series, Part I, Summer 1969, pp. 30-42.
[2] Nial Osborough, *op. cit.*
[3] See Chapter IV for precise data on this subject.
[4] Cf. R. Parant, R. Gilg and J. A. Clarence, 'Le Code penal camerounais—Code africain et franco-anglais', *Rév. sc. crim.*, 1967, note, p. 369.

On an international level, we would mention the European convention on the supervision of conditionally sentenced or conditionally released offenders, drawn up by the Council of Europe, which is intended to facilitate the granting of suspension to foreign nationals.[1]

PRESENT SYSTEMS

In most countries many legislative reforms have modified the original texts, complementing the ordinary suspended sentence either by a régime inspired by probation, or by suspension of the imposition of sentence, or again, as in the socialist countries, by a combination of measures involving control by the community. Often, as for example in the West German Penal Code, modified by the law of 1953 or in Portugal after the 1939 reform, the same text allows the judge to apply ordinary suspended sentence or suspension with *mise à l'épreuve* so that the two measures are frequently confused in statistics. In some countries—Israel for example—the two can be combined. Sometimes, too, the possibility of ordinary suspension exists theoretically, but in judicial practice it has fallen into disuse. In other cases, though theoretically they have probation at their disposal, judges may hesitate to use it for lack of qualified personnel.

The lines between the different types of suspension are thus far from clearly defined. Nevertheless, in an attempt to schematize the problem to some extent, we can distinguish four groups of countries:

1. In some countries, notably Spain, Greece, Italy, Turkey, Egypt and most Latin American countries—only the ordinary suspended sentence exists as yet. However, reforms currently under consideration recommend the adoption of a régime of probation. Thus one of the motions at the Enrico de Nicola Seminar, held at Bellagio in May 1961, was for the introduction of probation in Italy. The draft of the Egyptian Penal Code similarly envisages measures of supervision and assistance.

2. In many countries the ordinary suspended sentence functions alongside suspension with *mise à l'épreuve*.

In West Germany, for instance, since the reform of 1953

[1] Cf. *Nouvelles du Conseil de l'Europe*, January, 1965, p. 2.

(Art. 23, 24 and 25 of the Penal Code), there have been three types of suspension: ordinary suspended sentence, with no obligations or control; suspended sentence with obligations imposed on the convicted person under the control of the court; and suspended sentence with obligations and the supervision and assistance of a probation officer. Article 41 of the Swiss Penal Code allows the judge to 'put the offender under patronage'. The same is true of Portugal, since 1939 (see Art. 88–89 of the Penal Code). In the Netherlands probation is widely applied. Four reforms have already taken place in Japan since the law which introduced the suspended sentence in 1905. The suspended sentence was complemented by probation, first of all for political prisoners in 1936, then for 'offenders under ordinary law' in 1949. In Chile suspension with *mise à l'épreuve* was introduced alongside the ordinary suspended sentence in 1944, control being exercised by supervision of the convicted persons. Two countries have adopted the suspended sentence after adopting probation: Northern Ireland and Israel.

3. A new type of suspension—suspension of the imposition of sentence—has been introduced into the Scandinavian legal systems during the past few years. In Denmark, the court has the choice between suspending imposition of the sentence, and suspending execution of the sentence, and the latter can be an ordinary suspension or one accompanied by obligations and measures of supervision. The new Swedish Penal Code, which was passed in 1962 and came into force in 1965, states in the first article of Chapter XXVII that suspension of the imposition of sentence could be used 'if, after careful consideration of the character of the accused it seemed justifiable to say that supervision or any more serious measure of intervention would not be necessary in order to stop him from committing a further offence'. This measure cannot be used if the interests of general prevention or the seriousness of the offence stand in the way. At the same time, it can be linked with a definite sentence to a maximum penalty of 120 day fines.

4. In countries which come under the influence of the legal system of the USSR, the ordinary suspended sentence has tended to fall into disuse. Probation is the important thing—probation often accompanied by measures entailing supervision by the work community. In this way the 'court of comrades' constituted

by the workmates of the offender is substituted for the traditional conditional sentence. In the new code of East Germany of July 1968, we find a complete scale of measures (Art. 30–37) designed to avoid sentences of loss of liberty and ranging from suspension with obligation to work locally under supervision of the factory community, to public blame. The new Bulgarian Penal Code, which came into operation in June 1968, similarly advocates supervision by the community.

THE TECHNIQUE OF THE SUSPENDED SENTENCE

A brief look at the factors which characterize the suspended sentence in various countries might help us to see the different variations more clearly.

We shall study here the working of suspension in general, without going into details about the special rules which some countries—notably West Germany, Argentina and Switzerland—have drawn up for minors.

Categories of offender eligible for suspended sentence

Since the original aim of the suspended sentence was to avoid the bad influence of a short-term prison sentence on a person considered capable of improvement, most legal systems at first reserved the benefit of conditional sentence for first offenders. But the definition of 'first offender' itself is variable and more or less strict according to the country. At the present time, the tendency of criminal policy is to extend the benefit of the suspended sentence even to recidivists.

As a rule it is only sentences imposed by the national courts which are taken into account in the imposition of suspended sentences. Nevertheless, in 1892 Luxembourg specified that the judgements of foreign courts should also be taken into account and in 1940 the Brazilian Penal Code likewise referred to sentences imposed by foreign courts as bars to suspended sentence. Article 41 of the Swiss Penal Code specifies that the convicted man must not, during the previous five years, have undergone a sentence involving loss of liberty either in Switzerland or elsewhere. In countries where the law makes no mention of sentences imposed abroad, but where the granting of suspended sentence depends on the outcome of a personality investigation, foreign convictions are, in an indirect way, taken into account.

Many countries will still allow the offender to benefit from a suspended sentence only if he has incurred no previous conviction for crime or offence. This is so notably in Spain, Italy, Greece and the majority of the Latin American countries.

Elsewhere this idea is more flexibly applied and only convictions during the previous five years are counted (West Germany, Finland, Japan, Norway and Switzerland, among others).

Some legal systems even consider as first offenders persons who have previously incurred a penalty of six months or less (West Germany, Belgium, Finland). The Rumanian Code of 1968 specifies that offences committed during minority are not to be taken into account. In some countries—particularly Denmark and Sweden—it is now possible to apply the suspended sentence even to recidivists. In Japan recidivists can benefit from the conditional sentence, but stricter conditions have been laid down for them. In the draft penal code drawn up by Professor Eduardo Correia for Portugal, the benefit of the suspended sentence is no longer reserved for first offenders.

Let us remember, also, that most countries state, as a condition for receiving a suspended sentence, that the convicted man must be amenable to improvement, a factor which is assessed according to his background and character. The Swiss Penal Code, for example, specifies that the judge may suspend the execution of a sentence 'if the background and character of the convicted man indicate that this measure will deter him from further offences'.

In the USSR suspension can be granted only if 'the degree of danger to society which the convicted person presents does not necessitate his being isolated or carrying out corrective labour', in Italy 'if it can be assumed that the offender will not commit further offences'. Habitual or professional offenders are thus expressly excluded by law in certain cases (in this connection see Art. 61 of the Polish Penal Code, for example). In Hungary the Supreme Court excludes from the application of suspension offenders who present a serious social danger and 'persons who have committed offences for motives which are in keeping with their former social class or with their hostile feelings towards the socialist régime'.[1]

This evaluation of the individual assumes that the judge holds an investigation into his personality even if the law does not expressly provide for it. In Poland the recommendations of the Supreme Court emphasize the need for the court to gather together all relevant information, and in West Germany some jurists would wish to see investigations into personality figure among proposed reforms.

The offence and its sanctions

1. *Deprivation of liberty.* The offence which has led to the sentence must not, as a rule, be of such a serious nature that the culprit is thought to be incapable of improvement. The criterion most often chosen by the legislator is the length of the sentence incurred for the offence, and the maximum varies from one system to another, ranging from four months in Panama to five years in Austria. It is six months in Turkey and in Ecuador, nine months in West Germany (sentences to forced labour are excluded, and no limit is laid down for imprisonment for very minor breaches). The maximum is one year in Spain, Finland, Hungary, Greece, Italy (solitary confinement or imprisonment), Norway, the Netherlands and Switzerland; two years in Argentina (excluding sentences to solitary confinement), Brazil, Poland, Rumania and Czechoslovakia; three in Belgium, Bulgaria and Costa Rica. In Japan, following the 1947 reform, the field of application of the suspended sentence was extended to sentences of imprisonment or solitary confinement up to three years, so that suspension might be pronounced there even for murder.

Besides the maximum applicable as a general rule, in some legal systems we find a special rule for certain offences or certain categories of persons.

Thus in Italy the maximum for minors and for persons of over seventy is raised from one to two years and in Turkey from six months to a year.

In Norway the court has discretion to apply suspension to

[1] Cf. Tibor Horvat, 'La condamnation conditionnelle en droit pénal hongrois' in *Symposium international sur des problèmes du droit pénal socialiste,* Sofia, 1968, p. 90.

sentences over the maximum of two years recommended as a general rule. In Spain (Art. 93 of the Penal Code), if certain extenuating circumstances exist, the maximum can be as much as two years instead of one. In Hungary the penal code of 1961 allows suspension of sentences of one year as a general rule, but in certain specified cases, also sentences of two years.

On the other hand, in Rumania, for offences against public property, or where there are multiple offences, the maximum is reduced from two years to one year.

Some countries also exclude offences against public order (West Germany), or presenting a danger to society (Bulgaria) or, as in Ecuador, offences committed by civil servants in the execution of their duty.

Further legislative provisions may also restrict the application of suspension by expressly excluding certain offences. This is often the case for trafficking in drugs or tax evasion. Examples in other spheres include Poland's law of 22nd May 1958 relating to the repression of hooliganism and that of 18th June 1958 relating to offences against public property (on the latter, however, the courts are inclined not to observe the letter of the law). In Israel there was law No. 5722 of 1962 modifying the penal law relating to prostitution, in Greece the decree No. 4000 of 31st October 1959 relating to the delinquency of 'teddy boys', and in Portugal decree No. 46939 of 6th April 1966 on illegal emigration.

The tendency today, in most countries, is towards including longer sentences within the scope of suspension. Thus the Special Commission on penal law of the Bundestag in West Germany has recommended the extension of suspension to sentences of one year in a draft code. An alternative proposition (AE 1966) included sentences of two years.

2. *Fines*. Sometimes legislators, considering the essential aim of the suspended sentence to be the avoidance of the consequences of short-term prison sentences, exclude fines from its field of application. At other times, stressing the intimidating effect of the threat of revocation, they include fines among the penalties eligible for suspension. In the latter case, the maximum may be fixed by law or may be left to the discretion of the judge.

Fines are excluded from suspension in West Germany, Argentina, Brazil, Colombia, Spain, Northern Ireland, Israel, Mexico, Sweden and Switzerland.

On the other hand, the following countries permit fines to be conditionally suspended: Costa Rica, Ecuador, Finland, Hungary, Italy, Japan, Luxembourg, the Netherlands, Portugal, Rumania, Uruguay and Yugoslavia. In Japan only first offenders are eligible for suspension of a fine (the maximum being fixed at 25,000 yen), and for persistent offenders suspension cannot be granted.

At the present time this question is the subject of controversy in several countries. Argentina decided against inclusion of fines in suspension by law No. 17567 of 6th December 1967, applicable from 1st April 1968, which excludes monetary penalties from benefit of conditional suspension. In his draft of the Portuguese penal code, Professor Eduardo Correia—going back to the original text of the 1893 law—also reserves suspension for sentences to loss of liberty.[1] On the other hand Professor Schultz recommended that the Swiss law should allow fines to be included in the field of application of suspension.[2]

3. *Preventive measures, accessory penalties.* Certain legal systems, bearing in mind that preventive measures deal with an offender's state of 'dangerousness', exclude them from benefit of suspension. This is the case in West Germany and Rumania. But other countries leave the decision to the discretion of the court.

Two systems exist, also, for accessory penalties. Thus in Italy and Czechoslovakia suspension does not extend to accessory penalties. Similarly, Article 97 of the Spanish code specifies: 'conditional sentence shall not exempt from the penalties of suspension of the right to vote, or restrictions on the exercise of a public office or function, when these appear as accessory penalties'. The opposite system is illustrated by Swiss law, Article 41 stating: 'In case of sentence to a term of imprisonment not exceeding one year, to detention or to an accessory penalty, the judge may suspend execution of the penalty. . . .'

Suspension generally applies to the entire penalty. There is an exception to this rule in Denmark, however, where the court can grant suspension for a part of the sentence only, provided that the part which is executed does not exceed by more than three months the part which is suspended. In Israel, if suspension is

---

[1] Cf. Eduardo Correia 'Codigo penal, projecto da parte geral', 1963 offprint from *Boletim do Ministerio da Justica*, No. 127.
[2] Cf. 'Le sursis en droit suisse', *Rev. sc. crim.*, 1965, especially p. 819.

granted for the second time, it cannot be applied to the entire sentence.

OPERATIONAL PERIOD

To determine the operational period, the legislator can follow one of the following systems:
1. The operational period, as in the Bérenger law, is of a fixed length. In Latin America we find the longest periods—fixed at seven years in Costa Rica, five years in Peru and Uruguay, four years in Argentina. In Mexico it is only three years, and in Guatemala and the Republic of Panama, two years. In Egypt it is fixed by law at three years.

A variant of this system is that the operational period differs according to the category of the offence, which already tends to individualize the measure a bit more. In Italy and in Luxembourg the period is two years in the case of a minor breach and five years for the more serious offence of *délit*; in Turkey it is one year for a minor breach and five years for a rather more serious offence. In Rumania the length of the operational period is two years, plus the length of the sentence which has been pronounced.

2. The legislator allows wider discretionary power to the court, but nevertheless limits it between a fixed minimum and maximum. This is the system which is most frequently used at present. In Japan, Czechoslovakia, USSR and Yugoslavia, the operational period is of a minimum of one year and a maximum of five. In Austria and Israel the minimum is one year, but the maximum is only three. Most countries—West Germany, Bulgaria, Colombia, Spain, Finland, Norway, Portugal, Switzerland—have fixed the minimum at two years and the maximum at five. Although the minimum is two years in Brazil, the maximum is six. In Greece on the other hand, the minimum is three years and the maximum five. In Hungary, for a sentence to loss of liberty of one year or less, the operational period is three years at the most, and for sentences of more than one year it can go up to five years.

3. A minimum operational period is fixed by law, but it is left to the discretion of the court to modify it subsequently. Thus, in the Netherlands the period is theoretically three years in the

case of a more serious offence and two years for a minor breach, but the court can shorten or lengthen it subsequently.

Great flexibility is also apparent in the Danish system, where the court has the power to decide the length of the operational period. As a rule this must not be more than three years, but if particular circumstances dictate it, it can be prolonged to not more than five years. In Sweden, Article 3 of Chapter XXVII of the penal code lays down two years for the operational period, but, under Article 6, this can be taken to three years if the behaviour of the accused subsequently demands it. In Israel the court has the power to allot part of the operational period to probation and part to the ordinary suspended sentence.

OBLIGATIONS IMPOSED

Certain conditions can be imposed on the offender—the most frequent being reparation for damage caused. When these obligations become more complex, probationary control is necessary.

As an example, we can quote, among the countries which still have only the ordinary suspended sentence, the Italian Penal Code which, in Article 165, states: 'The conditional suspension of a sentence can be made dependent on the obligation to make restitution, on the payment of the sum fixed as reparation for damages or the sum provisionally awarded of the total amount of damages, and on the publication of the sentence as reparation of damage'.

THE GRANTING OF A SUSPENDED SENTENCE

As a general rule, when the appropriate conditions are fulfilled, this is left to the discretion of the court.

In Spain, however, there are two cases where a suspended sentence loses its optional character and becomes obligatory. The first (Art. 94) is when the sentence 'would have met most of the conditions required for exemption from responsibility under the rules laid down by this present Code', and the second case is where 'an offender has been prosecuted at the victim's request, and the said victim asks expressly that the suspended sentence be granted'.

Sometimes legislative provisions specify the conditions under which suspension can be granted for a second time. In West Germany this granting of a second suspended sentence is possible only if the first conditional sentence goes back more than five years (Art. 23, para 3). In Argentina, where formerly suspension could be granted only once, Law No. 17567 of December 1967 stated that a suspended sentence could be accorded a second time provided a period of eight years had passed since the first conditional sentence.

In some countries where ordinary suspended sentence and probation operate side by side, the court can be required to choose probation; this is the case in Japan when conditional sentence is granted for the second time.

Many legislative provisions require the reasons for the decision to be stated, as did the French law of 1891. Among these are the Swiss Penal Code (Art. 41, figure 2), the Greek Penal Code (Art. 100) and the Rumanian Penal Code (Art. 81).

REVOCATION

Revocation can be either obligatory or optional.

In many countries it is automatically applied by law in the case of a serious offence, but becomes optional if a minor breach is involved. Some countries demand that the second offence be of the same nature as the first if the revocation is to be obligatory. Thus, in Italy (Art. 168 of Penal Code) the suspension of sentence is legally revoked when, during the operational period, the convicted person commits an offence or contravention of the same kind, or fails to carry out the obligations which have been imposed on him. In Poland revocation is obligatory if the new offence is inspired by the same motives or is in the same category as the preceding one.

Other countries lay emphasis also on the intentional character of the offence. Thus, in West Germany, in Switzerland and in Bulgaria, the new offence must be committed intentionally for revocation to take place automatically by law.

The discovery of facts which would have been grounds for refusing a suspended sentence can also make revocation obligatory (West Germany, Japan).

In Scandinavia—Norway as well as Denmark and Sweden—

revocation is never obligatory and is left entirely to the discretion of the court.

THE EFFECTS OF A SUSPENDED SENTENCE

When the operational period has passed without revocation, in some countries (after the model of Bérenger's law) the sentence is erased; in others only the threat of execution of the sentence disappears and the judicial effects remain.

In the first group, for example, are Switzerland, where the judge orders the 'striking through of the court records', Poland and Japan, where the conviction is also considered null and void and is not taken into account for recidivism.

In the second group, among others, are Greece and West Germany, where it is considered that the penalty has been remitted, but that the judgement is not erased.

Sometimes the point is debatable. For instance, in Argentina, Article 27 of the Penal Code, stating that 'the sentence shall be considered as not having been imposed' has been interpreted in various ways. According to the interpretation which prevailed in the end, the effects of the judgement other than the actual execution of the sentence remain in force.

THE APPLICATION OF THE SUSPENDED SENTENCE

In most countries the suspended sentence still represents a basic element of penal policy. Even where probation exists, it continues to be used, showing itself a very useful complement to other institutions. In 1950 the Court of Criminal Appeal in Northern Ireland, when asked to declare the recorded sentence invalid, refused to uphold such a move and justified their decision by saying that the measure performed a useful function of individual prevention and was in keeping with the requirements of the penal law.[1]

While introducing reforms on particular points, the legislators have left the basic structure of the suspended sentence unchanged both in Argentina (Law 17567 of 6th December 1967) and in Rumania, where, and this is worthy of note, it is written into the

[1] Nial Osborough, *op. cit.*, p. 30.

new penal code which came into force in June 1968, Section III of Chapter V, entitled 'Individualization of sentences'.

In West Germany, although some penologists stress the need to make more use of probation, the courts continue to apply the ordinary suspended sentence very widely. It is the same in Switzerland. In Spain a suspended sentence can be considered automatic once the required conditions are fulfilled. In Portugal, where there are not yet sufficient social workers to make probation practicable, the suspended sentence is used very frequently, especially for minors.[1] In Poland about half of the sentences of two years or less benefit from suspension, in spite of reminders to the courts from the Supreme Court that they have other methods at their disposal.

In the Near East, Israel has opened the way to new combinations by introducing the ordinary suspended sentence into the probation system, and in the Far East, Japan, showing a bold spirit of innovation, permits suspension to be granted in the majority of cases.

---

[1] J. G. Lopes 'Le traitement des jeunes adultes délinquants au Portugal', *Boletim da Administraccâo penitenciaria*, No. 16, 1965, p. 20.

IV

Judicial Practice and the Results of the Suspended Sentence

THE study of judicial practice and of the results of the suspended sentence is undoubtedly hindered by inadequate criminological documentation and by statistics whose gaps have often been pointed out. On two essential points, information is extremely sketchy—the influence of the personality of offenders on the use of the suspended sentence and the effectiveness of the method. Despite the limited significance of observations made in these circumstances, we believe that it might be useful to discuss briefly what comes to light from examination of the data available to us.

THE USE OF THE SUSPENDED SENTENCE BY DIFFERENT JURISDICTIONS

FRANCE

Many factors have influenced the increase in the use that the courts make of the suspended sentence. We would mention particularly:

The type of jurisdiction (assize courts, *tribunaux correctionnels*, police courts, juvenile courts). A complex combination of factors operates here: the gravity of the offence, the age of the offender, differences in the composition of the jurisdictions and the procedures followed, and in the training of the judges, their psychology, etc.

The type of penalty: imprisonment or fine.
The kind of offence.
Length of sentence.
Use of remand.
Personality of the offenders.
Locality, that is, regional differences in the nature of crime

and in social reaction to crime, such as the differences between a large town with a busy and important court and the little country courts which are hardly used at all.

Time, in other words all the social changes in the conception of punishment, in the organization of justice and in the ordinary man himself. The introduction of a kind of probation into the Code of penal procedure in France in 1958, under the form of *'sursis avec mise à l'épreuve'* is a fact which necessarily influenced the use of the ordinary suspended sentence.

The granting of suspended sentence by the different jurisdictions

Before interpreting the statistics here, we must make a preliminary statement. To appreciate the variations between jurisdictions in the application of the Bérenger law, it would be necessary to be able to compare the number of suspended sentences granted with the number of sentences eligible for suspension, that is sentences upon persons 'not having previously been sentenced to imprisonment or to a more serious penalty for a crime under ordinary law'. Now, judicial statistics are organized in such a way that they do not permit us to isolate this factor, and so we are reduced to comparing the number of suspended sentences granted with the total number of sentences of imprisonment, instead of with the total of sentences eligible for suspension.

Taking this point into account, the data which we present as an appendix to this study reveal clear enough variations in the use of the suspended sentence, as a function of the type of jurisdiction. For one year (1964) we see that, in relation to the prison sentences imposed, suspension was granted in 25·3 per cent of cases by the Assizes (see Table 1), in 38·8 per cent of cases by the *tribunaux correctionnels* and the appeal courts, and in 39·3 per cent of cases by the police courts (see Table 2). These last deal with *contraventions* of the 5th class (that is, *contraventions* which were created in 1959 by giving to certain *délits* the character of *contraventions* and which are eligible for benefit from suspension, whilst judicial interpretations inspired by the preparatory work of the *loi Bérenger* had decided that suspension was inapplicable to imprisonment and fines pronounced for *contraventions de simple police*). The juvenile courts (see Table 3) granted suspension in 74·1 per cent of cases.

JUDICIAL PRACTICE AND SUSPENDED SENTENCE 55

Each of these jurisdictions, if we go back to before the two world wars, has evolved its own pattern of suspended sentences. The Assize Courts, which used to show a marked reluctance to grant suspension of prison sentences, before the first world war, with a percentage of 10 per cent, finally arrived at the percentage we have quoted above. This represents a genuine stabilization in the figure, since in 1966 it always hovered around 20 per cent, while the figures for the *tribunaux correctionnels* and the appeal courts decreased or increased. So far as the juvenile courts are concerned, from 1956 to 1964 the figures show that although the total of prison sentences considerably increased (going from 771 to 6,820), the proportion of suspended sentences remained fairly stable, around 65 per cent, increasing from 1963 and 1964 to account for three-quarters of the sentences (see Table 3). The way suspensions of fines have evolved is very significant. The rate of suspension was very high, around 40 per cent, from 1909 to 1930. The Report of the Ministry of Justice at this time underlined this striking percentage, and suggested that there was an abuse of the law as regards this type of penalty. In the period 1956 to 1964 there was a marked diminution of the percentage, which in nine years passed from 17 per cent to 5·6 per cent (see Table 4).

The data on the granting of suspended sentences of imprisonment according to region are difficult to analyse, because of the more complex factors involved—population, habits, judicial practice, etc. So, we prefer to confine ourselves here to a comparison between the use of the suspended sentence in the important courts and that in the courts of small towns which come under the same Court of Appeal, because that will enable us to judge the reaction of the jurisdictions in terms of the social facts which confront them. The living conditions in the big towns, on the one hand, and the greater volume of crime on the other, seem *a priori* to predispose the larger courts to adopt a more restrictive policy in the matter of suspension of imprisonment. The figures for 1964 (see Table 5) appear to confirm this hypothesis, and it is striking to note that the rate of suspension is appreciably less high in every case in the courts of the large towns than in those of the smaller towns coming under the same Court of Appeal.

Suspensions of prison sentences in terms of the nature of the offence

The type of offence constitutes a factor for or against the granting of a suspended sentence, and the statistics for the years 1956 to 1964 shed an interesting light on this point. The two extremes were unintentional wounding, where the rate borders on 70 per cent and the 'vagrancy/begging' category where it is of the order of 3–5 per cent. Between these fall drunken driving, with between 55 and 62 per cent, offences against public decency, with 50 to 57 per cent (note the spectacular drop in 1957 to 30 per cent), dishonoured cheques and desertion of family, with a rate of 40 per cent (the rate of ordinary suspended sentences for the latter offence dropped after an increase in 1960 (54 per cent), while the rate of suspension with *mise à l'épreuve* increased). Finally, larceny and breach of trust follow very similar curves, fluctuating around 35 per cent; obtaining by false pretences comes between 25 and 30 per cent (see Table 6c).

Length of sentence

Suspension of imprisonment is more or less easily granted, according to the length of sentence. Thus, in 1964, out of a total of 47,029 impositions of suspended prison sentences, 81·9 per cent were of three months or less, only 15·3 per cent were of more than three months but less than one year, and only 2·8 per cent were more than one year's imprisonment (see Table 7). In relation to preceding years, these figures reveal that judicial practice has hardly varied, except where sentences of more than one year are concerned, where suspension used to be granted much less frequently (0·6 per cent as opposed to 2·8 per cent).

We should examine here, at the same time as length of sentence, the length of time that the accused may have been held on remand in custody, because the two factors are often linked in the minds of judges when they are considering whether to grant suspension of imprisonment.

In fact, as it happens, a suspended sentence may be more easily granted in some cases in consideration of the length of time that the offender has been held on remand in custody.

When this waiting period appears to be sufficiently long, the court may be tempted to choose between two solutions: to fix the length of the sentence (without suspension) in such a way as to 'cover' the remand in custody, or to grant suspension while making the sentence longer than that of the remand, so as to preserve the intimidating effect of suspension.

In any case, it must not be forgotten that the suspended sentence, even if it retains its intimidating value, does not always fulfil its other role, which is to protect the offender from dangerous contact with prison. From a sample survey of 588 cases which we carried out (to fill the gap in official information on this point), it appeared that a suspended sentence of imprisonment was preceded by remand in custody in a quarter of the cases (25·2 per cent). The length of this remand was less than three weeks in 13·6 per cent and more than three weeks in 11·6 per cent.

The personality of the offender

As early as 1909 the inaugural report of the *Compte de la justice criminelle* stated that criminal judges were concerned too much with the nature of the incriminating act. It was the personality of the offender which should be the essential consideration by virtue of which a suspended sentence was granted or refused. We have certainly evolved in this direction, but official information—despite reforms undertaken by the Ministry of Justice to give criminal statistics a criminological and juridical content—fails to tell us to what extent judges are at present basing their decision to grant suspension on the personality of the offender, his social situation and the prospects of recidivism or of his rehabilitation in society which can be deduced from his file and from discussions. However, two basic facts can be examined—the age and the sex of the offenders.

While the curve of the suspended sentence for men has kept fairly steady since 1960 at around 36 per cent, that for women is on average 60 per cent (see Tables 8 and 9). Thus, we can say that it is between one and a half times and twice as easy for a woman to receive a suspended sentence than for a man. If we take both age and sex into account, we see that the preference given to women is strongest towards the age of thirty; no doubt the fact that they have young children in their care plays a considerable part in this.

If we take age alone, the frequency of suspended sentence is highest (50 per cent) at 18, decreases up to 26 (34·7 per cent) and thereafter remains steady at about 35 per cent until around 30; it then increases progressively, at 60 years reaching the same frequency as at 18 and even overtaking it. It will be noted that the drop is steep from 19 to 21 years, when the preferential treatment of minors of 18 ends, and less steep beyond penal majority, while the increase after 30 is very slow and progressive (see Tables 9 and 10).

The incidence of suspension with mise à l'épreuve

The introduction into French law of suspension with *mise à l'épreuve* by the code of penal procedure 1958, Article 738, has necessarily had an effect on the use of the ordinary suspended sentence.

The two variations of the penalty are not entirely competitive, since the conditions for granting what we now call probation are broader than those for an ordinary suspended sentence.

An examination of the records of offenders given probation (Table 11) throws into relief the fact that offenders who had previously had suspended sentences make up 20 to 25 per cent of the total, and that those who had previously been imprisoned make up about 10 per cent; first offenders, who are the only ones for whom the two measures compete, form 65 to 70 per cent of the total of probationers.

The choice which the court has, in the case of first offenders, between ordinary suspended sentence and suspension with *mise à l'épreuve* might conceivably have caused a falling off in the number of ordinary suspended sentences, proportionate to the growing use of probation. Some writers even predicted a rapid decline in the suspended sentence.

No such thing occurred. On the contrary, statistics show that there were more suspended sentences after the introduction of probation. Perhaps we might be permitted to draw the conclusion that the climate of thought which led to this innovation benefited every form of suspended prison sentence by emphasizing once again the unfortunate consequences of imprisonment which, for so many offenders, lessen the chances of 'going straight'.

The graphs which we have drawn up (see, for example, Graph 4 for a breakdown by sex, or Graphs 1, 2 and 3 for the different offences) show, nevertheless, that the increase in the rate of ordinary suspended sentences, which became noticeable from 1959, did not continue beyond 1961.

Probation developed until that time only very slowly and cautiously, its progress being considerably hampered by the shortage of qualified staff to put the measure into practice; its incidence is still only a tenth of that of the ordinary suspended sentence. But its powers of expansion are considerable, and if the necessary staff can be obtained, we predict that it will be increasingly used and that it will encroach a great deal more upon the field of ordinary suspension. This can already be seen in relation to certain offences, such as desertion of the family; here the obvious decrease in the rate of suspended sentences since 1960 seems to correspond very precisely with the rapid increase in the granting of suspension with *mise à l'épreuve*.

To make it possible to demarcate clearly the field of application of the ordinary suspended sentence (which undoubtedly has its advantages for certain categories of offender), and that of suspension with *mise à l'épreuve* (which is to be recommended for others), we hope that in future statistics will be so presented as to enable us to determine, in a rather more scientific way, their respective effectiveness in relation to each category of convicted person.

OTHER COUNTRIES

We have very limited information at our disposal if we wish to study judicial practice in other countries which have adopted the suspended sentence. Moreover, it is often difficult to distinguish suspended sentences, properly so-called, from forms which are more related to probation, either because of the imposition of particular obligations, or because of measures of aid or supervision. Thus the figures quoted in the tables can give no more than indications. Nevertheless, they do reveal significant differences in the importance placed on the suspended prison sentence in different countries, the figures varying between 11 and 61 per cent of the total prison sentences imposed upon adults.

At the top we find two people's democracies, Yugoslavia and Poland, where the percentages of conditional sentences are more than half the total number of prison sentences: for the former, 61 per cent in 1964, and for the latter 55 per cent in 1963 (see Tables 13 and 14). In Poland we see a tendency to a continuous increase in the number of suspensions in relation to a very high number of prison sentences. The courts have the power to combine suspension with supervision (Art. 62–1 Penal Code) or with an obligation to compensate (Art. 62–2 Penal Code), but these powers are used only rarely. This caused the Supreme Court, in 1957, to censure the courts severely, accusing them of using a measure automatically, without thorough examination of the personality of the offender, and forgetting the possibilities offered by Article 62. The practice of suspending sentences is, for certain offenders, much more liberal than was anticipated by the legislators. In fact, the law of 22nd May 1958 on increased penal responsibility for hooliganism, and that of 18th June 1959 on offences against public property, state that suspension shall be granted for these two categories only in exceptional circumstances. But the courts interpret the text so liberally that the percentage of suspended sentences for hooligans and for those guilty of embezzlement of public funds, is hardly lower than the general average.

Japan is another country where suspension is in great favour, even if it is not quite true to say, like Tsuneo Kikkawa, that its use there is so extensive that it was unmatched by any other country.[1] Before the second world war it already represented 16 to 17 per cent of the total prison sentences; after the war, the rise in offences and prison sentences was accompanied—partly to remedy the overcrowding problem in prisons—by a trebling in the use of suspension, under its twofold form of ordinary suspended sentence and suspension with probation (introduced in 1936 for political prisoners, then in 1949 for offenders under ordinary law, and in 1954 made obligatory by law when suspension was applied for the second time). Of the total of suspensions, ordinary suspended sentences represented around 80 per cent and probation 20 per cent. In 1964, 43·5 per cent of sentences of solitary confinement and long-term imprisonment were imposed with ordinary suspension, and in 1965 this percentage was over 44·2 per cent (see Table 15).

[1] Tsuneo Kikkawa 'Le sursis à l'exécution des peines, en particulier l'amende, au Japon' in *Rev. int. dr. pén.*, 1967, pp. 49–61.

JUDICIAL PRACTICE AND SUSPENDED SENTENCE 61

In Belgium the statistics show a steady increase in the use of suspended sentences by the *tribunaux correctionnels* which, since 1959, have arrived at the point where suspension was granted in more than half of all cases (see Table 16).

In West Germany statistics for the whole of the Federal Republic are difficult to analyse, because the three forms of *Strafaussetzung zur Bewährung* (ordinary suspension, a variation which comprises obligations, and which is combined with obligations and the aid of a probation officer) are not put under separate headings. However, special inquiries made in Hanover and in Prussia indicate a rate of application of ordinary suspended sentences of 30 to 34 per cent, slightly less than in the French courts (39 per cent).

In Italy and Spain we would point out the automatic way in which a suspended sentence is granted by the courts when the legal conditions are fulfilled. It all takes place as if the suspension were granted *ope legis* and not *ope judice*.

In relation to the total number of prison sentences, the number of suspensions in Italy represents a percentage which increased to 45·2 per cent in 1964.

According to Professor Inkeri Anttila,[1] suspension is used in Finland much more frequently today than it was previously: it is granted to one man in six sentenced to solitary confinement, to one man in three sentenced to imprisonment: a rate of suspension for serious offences of about 33 per cent.

Among the countries with a more restrictive policy towards the suspended sentence, we can quote Egypt, where the rate is a little less than 27 per cent; Israel, where, taking probation and suspended sentence together, only 14 per cent benefited from the conditional sentence in 1963; and Greece, where the percentage of suspended prison sentences was between 11·3 and 13·5 per cent in the last three years (see Tables 17–20).

THE RESULTS OF THE SUSPENDED SENTENCE

The effectiveness of the suspended sentence cannot be deduced from a simple statistical comparison of the rate of recidivism in respect of persons who have undergone their sentences and those

[1] *The Trend of Criminal Policy in the Finnish Legal System*, Helsinki, 1966.

whose sentences have been suspended. In fact suspension is granted by reason of a combination of favourable circumstances, which may relate either to the comparatively minor nature of the offence, or to the personality of the offender, and offer a good prognosis for his future behaviour. This selective element in the application of the suspended sentence makes a general comparison valueless.

Moreover, the effectiveness of the measure can be assessed only in relation to each category of offender. And different offenders react differently to a suspended sentence.

Before 1930, the Official Statistics gave the number of revocations of suspended prison sentences for the year, set out according to the year the sentence had been pronounced. Therefore, we know the rate of revocation of suspensions which was, before the 1914–1918 war, generally less than 10 per cent, and which in 1922 went down to 6·8 per cent (see Table 12).

This information has, unfortunately, since been dropped from the Official Statistics, and we have no means of knowing the currect rate of revocation of suspensions.

To rectify this we have carried out a survey[1] in three *tribunaux correctionnels* of varying size. One is in the south of France (Toulon), one in the Paris area (Troyes) and the third in the north (Lille), giving a total sample of 588 suspended sentences of imprisonment, out of which 515, 87·6 per cent of the total, were ordinary suspended sentences, and 73, 12·4 per cent of the total, were suspension with *mise à l'épreuve* (probation). (This proportion is in keeping with the general figure for France.)

The amnesty of 18th June 1966 gave rise to difficulties in the compiling of statistics. So we have had to confine ourselves to sentences since the 8th January 1966. The sentences were taken from each of the chosen courts until they reached two hundred for each. These were taken from the court records, in chronological order and without discrimination. They represented a period of four months in Toulon, five and a half months at Troyes and one month at Lille. As we asked to see the judicial records at

---

[1] We should like to thank the following people for their co-operation: M. Carpentier, Head of the court's offices at Toulon; M. Larue, Public Prosecutor at Troyes; M. Bernard, examining magistrate in Lille; and M. Chirol, statistician at the Research Centre in Vaucresson. This study is still going on.

the end of 1967, the average operational period was about eighteen months.

The concept of *recidivism* was extended to all further sentences, to fines as well as to imprisonment, and was consequently wider than the idea of *revocation of suspension*, which is incurred only by a more serious sentence. Examination of the judicial records gave the following general figures:

	Ordinary suspended sentence	Probation	Suspended sentence and probation combined
Total	515	73	588
Recidivists	62	18	60
Percentage	12·0	24·6	13·6

Taking into account the calculations made previous to 1930, we have reason to think that this rate of recidivism of 12 per cent for the ordinary suspended sentence—taken over a period of eighteen months—represents 60 per cent of the recidivism during a five-year operational period.

By extrapolating on the legal period of five years, $\frac{12 \times 100}{60}$, we can thus consider the rate of recidivism to be 20 per cent.

This result—with the reservations imposed by the small size of the sample—seems to indicate an appreciable increase in recidivism in relation to the period before 1922 (when revocations never went beyond 10 per cent of cases).

It is also apparent that the figure of recidivism in the case of suspension with probation is twice as high as that for the ordinary suspended sentence. Here there is also an important difference between the courts; the rate of recidivism (for ordinary suspended sentence plus probation) was 9·3 per cent at Toulon, 18·9 per cent at Troyes and 12·4 per cent at Lille.

For a correct interpretation, these figures should be studied as a function of the different distribution of offences in the three courts, and according to the two categories of ordinary suspended sentence or probation.

In fact, we see considerable variations in the rate of recidivism according to the *nature of the offence*: 6·5 per cent for unintentional wounding, 14·2 per cent for larceny, 27·3 per cent for desertion of the family. Moreover, perpetrators of unintentional wounding represented 14 per cent of those sentenced at Toulon, 6·7 per cent at Lille and only 2·5 per cent at Troyes; similarly, thieves made up 18 per cent of the sample at Toulon, 39·4 per cent at Lille and 56·7 per cent at Troyes.

Other data confirm the general tendencies discovered by earlier studies; thus, distribution according to *sex*: 14 per cent recidivism for men and 2·3 per cent for women; according to *marital status*: 16·2 per cent recidivism for the unmarried and 10·1 per cent for the married; by *age*: from 18 to 29 years old the figure for recidivism goes from 24·5 per cent to 9·3 per cent, to increase again from 30 to 34 (16·7 per cent) and subsequently to drop to 7·6 per cent at 50.

Finally, another factor seems to us to demand closer examination. We became aware that the rate of recidivism varied considerably according to the length of *remand in custody*:

no remand in custody	11·8 per cent recidivism
less than three weeks in custody	15·0 per cent recidivism
more than three weeks in custody	23·5 per cent recidivism

In studying the application of the suspended sentence by the courts, we see considerable variations from one country to another. But although its frequency may vary significantly, it can nevertheless be claimed that nowhere has it fallen into disuse and that in some places its use is increasing. It is significant that in France, far from overshadowing the suspended sentence, probation has, on the contrary, brought it to the notice of the magistrates as a complementary instrument of criminal policy, the advantages of which have been proved over a century of judicial practice.

Comparative Conclusions

WE have discussed the suspended sentence in its historical context, as a working legal institution, and its geographical expansion. We should now like to give a broad view of its proper significance and its precise place in a system of criminal law in force.

As far as the significance and the objectives of the suspended sentence are concerned, we would stress once more that it is first and foremost an instrument of penal policy belonging, originally, to the Franco-Belgian system and embodying all that was understood by the term 'penal policy' in that system. Above and beyond all the controversies and technical juristic arguments which, it seems to us, are out of date nowadays, it should always be remembered that the suspended sentence was born in the countries of written law and strict legality, as a *conditional suspension of the penalty*, in the narrowest and most precise meaning of that phrase.

Having made this preliminary observation, we must acknowledge the fact that the suspended sentence has not remained in its pure state, even within the Franco-Belgian system. It has been periodically added to and has incorporated many elements from the system of probation. Today, even in its two countries of origin, it appears in a twofold form at least—that of the ordinary suspended sentence (the only one envisaged by Bérenger and Lejeune) and suspension with *mise à l'épreuve* which, clearly, is closely related to the probation system. Nevertheless, it was stated, and with some justification, in the French code of penal procedure of 1958 that suspension with *mise à l'épreuve* did not in fact constitute a true régime of probation, and this is probably true for most of the continental countries. Conditional sentence, even if it is combined with certain conditions or with a régime of supervision, always embodies the spirit of the original system of the ordinary suspended sentence. We must keep this in mind if we wish to understand the function of the conditional sentence in most of the positive legal systems of the present day.

If problems exist as to the significance and the import of the institution of the conditional sentence, there are still more problems when we look at the development of the suspended sentence, and what we have already said bears this out. Its development can be considered on three different levels: the national legislative level, the practical level and what we might call the scientific or general level.

From the legislative point of view, whether we look at the history or the geography of suspension, we see that its development has been dominated by the presence, not to say the competition, of the probation system and by the differences it has been possible to establish between the two institutions.

It is undeniable that since the beginning of the twentieth century, and particularly following the first world war, the suspended sentence has been very much influenced by the probation system. Attempts have been made to introduce many elements of probation into the system of suspended sentence but, precisely because, as we have said, that system is part of a régime of written law, this progressive introduction of probation has not been easy. We must also emphasize that, rather as in Bérenger and Lejeune's time, the jurists and legislators of the continent have seen probation less in terms of the English system, with its roots in the ancient contract of the recognizance, or in terms of efforts such as those of John Augustus in Boston in the nineteenth century, than in terms of the actual *laws* (in the continental sense of the word) which served to reaffirm, revive and reformulate the system in the United States or in England at the end of the last century and the beginning of this.

The story of the relations between the suspended sentence and probation would merit a whole study, on the level of the history of the institutions and almost of the comparative psychology of the different peoples. The continental countries have always sought to establish their new régime of conditional sentence without departing from the general principles of their legal systems and in conformity with the tradition of the civil-law countries. On this point, innovators on the continent have often had to struggle against the resistance of those who did not want to see any departure from the old perspectives, and who almost instinctively reacted against the idea of borrowing from an institution or tradition which was foreign and which seemed to them juridically heretical.

On the practical plane, the suspended sentence had first to become accepted and established, just as the measure of suspension with *mise à l'épreuve* is striving to become accepted and established in the continental countries today. Then it had to find its proper sphere of application. In the continental countries which have adopted the suspended sentence, three tendencies have been noticeable on the part of judges, and these have occasionally been somewhat contradictory.

The first has consisted in the increasing, almost automatic, application of the suspended sentence to every first offender who has committed a minor breach of law; the opponents of suspension (and there are still some, even though they may not openly declare themselves) have talked of a weakening of repression and protested at this so-called right to a suspended sentence which, they claimed, led to the first offence going unpunished. To which one might reply that if this so-called impunity, in fact this legal clemency, is not followed by any recidivism, then it is well and good that a first offence of a minor character can remain unsanctioned.

A second, more debatable tendency, has been for judges to grant a suspended sentence, but at the same time to make the penalty imposed more stringent. In this respect, on the level of judicial psychology or sociology, there has been a curious phenomenon: it has produced a reversal of the order of values envisaged by the original promoters of the suspended sentence. They wanted the judge first to lay down the extent of the penalty and fix it in an objective way. If this sentence permitted the granting of suspension, he could then consider whether conditional suspension of the sentence imposed should be accorded. However, the reverse has now come about. The judge begins by deciding whether he should grant suspension, that is to say whether or not he should send the accused to prison; if he decides to impose simply a conditional sentence, only then will he assess what sentence is appropriate. Thus, by distorting the original institution, the judge has actually raised the penalty pronounced. The judge is motivated by various considerations: most frequently he is concerned to make the threat more intimidating by a heavier sentence; occasionally to satisfy public opinion, which is sometimes more repressive than the judge himself and which, in many cases, desires a heavy penalty; and finally there is the desire, on the part of many judges, to stress the retributive character of the punishment, providing for the case when the offender, duly warned, nevertheless commits a further offence.

A last tendency is that which leads a judge to refuse suspended sentence in certain cases and for certain offences. Here again he has to take into account public opinion, which sometimes demands heavy penalties in the name of deterrence or what is called general prevention. This happens, for example, whenever offences by gangs of youths, or driving offences, show a dangerous increase. No doubt the judge's reaction is understandable, and in many cases justified, but if it is taken to extremes, there is a risk of stripping the conditional sentence of its character as an instrument of individualization.

The development of the suspended sentence calls for a few general or, if it is not too ambitious a word, scientific conclusions. We shall limit ourselves here to three very simple observations:

First, as we have already emphasized in the preceding chapters, the development of the conditional sentence has been hampered by a certain closeness to, and even a confusion with, probation. It has been hindered rather than helped by elements, often disparate, borrowed at random from the probation system without sufficient thought. The error has been to try to merge the two institutions instead of clearly defining the two in their respective fields.

In the continental legal systems or those inspired by them, the development of this measure has also been hindered by temporary and derogatory laws, which have been brought in in various countries and at various times to forbid, at least provisionally, the granting of suspended sentences for particular offences or to particular offenders. Although they purported to be provisional or exceptional, these legal dispensations did more than simply make the judges hesitant; they cast doubt on the legitimacy and permanence of the suspended sentence, which was no longer in force as a judiciary instrument of individualization.

Lastly, as we have seen, among the original objectives of the suspended sentence, was that of avoiding short-term prison sentences. Outside the system of suspended sentences, various procedures have appeared and developed in modern legal systems which have the same aim. In fact, looking at the history of penal institutions as a whole, we might ask whether the development of the suspended sentence has not been made more difficult in modern times by such measures. There has been, for example, 'weekend arrest', the development of the fine beyond its traditional framework, above all, the multiplication of disqualifications from the exercise of certain professions or certain activities. Finally, there are the possibilities of finding new methods: establishing, perhaps, short periods of confinement to serve as a psychological shock, which would obviously not entail suspension; perhaps régimes of work release, or semi-liberty, which it is hoped will avoid the bad effects of imprisonment, the very purpose for which the suspended sentence was originally designed.

A second general observation concerns the teleological aspect of this question; what degree of finality can be claimed for the imposition of the conditional sentence? Much was said, at one time, about the contrast between 'the suspended sentence as a favour', as laid down in the original Franco-Belgian legislation and 'the suspended sentence as treatment', as it was to develop later in more modern legislation, as for example the Swiss Penal Code of 1937. Although not entirely unjustified, this idea of contrast seems to us to be forcing the issue a little. Firstly, we can see that in 1888 or 1891 the notion of 'treatment of offenders' was practically unheard of and the problem consisted in devising ways of dispensing and grading traditional punishment so as to make it more beneficial both to society and to the offender. In the second place, in Bérenger's mind if not in Lejeune's, conditional sentence, by implication at least, was indeed a way of *treating* the offender, by a more developed system of individualization of punishment. From the moment we have got away from fixed penalties, or a judicial tariff laid down by law, it is indeed a problem of treatment that presents itself, even if it is not seen as such on the penological level. The bringing closer together of the suspended sentence and probation has emphasized this point of view, since the suspended sentence has become something more than the simple threat of ultimate execution of the sentence, and has been subordinated to certain conditions, and since the offenders have begun to be required to accept supervision and given assistance. So, it is not inaccurate to speak of an evolution from 'the suspended sentence as a favour' to 'the suspended sentence as treatment', nor to state that the influence of probation, its methods and its motives, have accelerated and emphasized this evolution. But we also believe that, once the break was accepted with actual retribution, and consequently with the inevitable imposition of a penalty by way of legal suffering in order to let the convicted man go free from the court, by offering him a chance to reinstate himself by his own good behaviour, we were already, and necessarily, within the system and the perspective of *treatment*. The contrast between the two ideas must not, therefore, be exaggerated, and we should remember that Bérenger's 'suspended sentence as a favour' recalled, although somewhat obscurely, that ancient contract of good behaviour which is at the basis of the probation system.

Thus, once again, we find ourselves led to a comparison of suspension and probation. On a general level, this time both scientific and legislative, it can be said that since the end of the nineteenth century, or since 1888 (the date of the first law on the conditional sentence), we have gone through three consecutive stages.

The first was that of opposition between probation and the suspended sentence; probation logically entailed not only suspension of the execution, but also of the imposition, of the sentence, and was accompanied by a system of supervision or assistance, two factors which the original suspended sentence ignored completely. Probation, then, was characteristic of the *common law* countries, while the suspended sentence was essentially an institution of the *civil law* system.

The second stage was that of the growing influence of probation on the suspended sentence, and the increasing closeness of the two systems. It is this that happened particularly during the period between the two world wars when, as we have already mentioned, many continental civil-law countries introduced elements of probation into the régime of the suspended sentence. Immediately after the second world war it was possible to anticipate that the two would become amalgamated in continental legislations, in such a way that probation would predominate. Some people even thought that the suspended sentence in its old form of a conditional threat would disappear completely. What further use, they argued, would there be for this over-simplified and incomplete system in the presence of a subtle and developed régime of *mise à l'épreuve*.

In fact this hasty conclusion was itself incomplete. An impartial examination of positive legislation would indicate that we are today going through a third stage, where the two institutions are once again becoming differentiated, and in which the suspended sentence retains, or rather regains, its originality and its former *finality* in contrast to probation. And it is in this desirable and differentiated coexistence that we can today discern the respective features of the two systems and judge their juridical and social significance.

These observations lead us naturally to the last point in these brief comparative conclusions. We must now try to characterize the place of the conditional sentence today in the systems of positive criminal law. If we refer to the most modern and most progressive system, i.e. that of Sweden, we must remember that the Franco-Belgian system of suspended sentence was introduced there in 1906, at the same time as conditional release. After that a series of reforms broadened the institution and made it more flexible, because of a concern for individualization, but also for practical effectiveness, which brought it much closer to probation. Here again, it seemed that the two systems might merge. However, the Swedish Penal Code of 1962 placed the two institutions firmly face to face, or rather side by side, each with its own role and its particular autonomy. This is what we find by studying successively Chapter XXVII, on the conditional sentence, and Chapter XXVIII, on probation. There has been a progress, by successive stages, from the pure suspended sentence, opposed to probation, through closer combinations of the two procedures, arriving in the end at the distinct conservation of the two methods of treating offenders, each fulfilling a different function.

It is with this, we feel, that we should conclude. After loudly affirming its originality, the conditional sentence has seemed gradually to shed it, only to rediscover it again in the present day. If we look at what might be called the existential reality of the suspended sentence, we see that, in a continuous perspective, it remains an instrument of criminal policy based on judicial individualization. But we must remember, on the other hand, that individualization today has taken on a new aspect. We are in an age in which more and more doubt is being cast on the efficacy, if not even the legitimacy, of imprisonment. It is an age in which methods of treatment in the open are being ceaselessly developed; and in which it is essential that the judge should have a flexible range of sanctions at his disposal. The choice is not only between confinement and total liberty, but even between these sanctions and a kind of help like that given to the minor or to the invalid. In a general climate of penal and penological thought which leans towards restoring a sense of responsibility to the individual's social behaviour, the suspended sentence, both in its old form and in its more differentiated modern forms, is a valid and sound method of non-institutional reaction against crime, based on consideration of the personality of the offender. It is because of this fact that, more than three-quarters of a century after its first appearance in continental law, it still holds a place of prime importance.

Statistical Appendix

Table 1. Suspended Prison Sentences in the Assizes

Year	Total sentences for criminal and minor offences	Total prison sentences	Imprisonment with ordinary suspended sentence		Imprisonment with suspension with mise à l'épreuve		Total of suspensions	
			No.	% of imprisonments	No.	% of imprisonments	No.	% of imprisonments
1912	2,150	1,105	116	10.5	—	—	116	10.5
1922	1,880	990	146	14.7	—	—	146	14.7
1930	1,103	596	87	14.6	—	—	87	14.6
1936	1,200	706	204	28.9	—	—	204	28.9
1956	1,057	600	229	38.2	—	—	229	38.2
1957	1,080	569	213	37.4	—	—	213	37.4
1958	1,072	495	175	35.4	—	—	175	35.4
1959	1,965	490	130	26.5	12	2.4	142	28.9
1960	914	459	135	29.4	18	3.9	143	33.3
1961	934	502	134	26.7	38	4.1	172	30.8
1962	1,038	543	136	25.0	42	7.7	178	32.7
1963	1,288	692	13	1.9	49	7.1	62	9.0
1964	1,341	608	154	25.3	35	4.0	189	29.3

Table 2. **The Suspension of Imprisonment before the Courts of Summary Jurisdiction, Police Courts and the Appeal Courts**

Year	Total of prison sentences	Ordinary suspended sentences		Suspension with mise à l'épreuve		Total of ordinary suspended sentences and suspension with mise à l'épreuve	
		No.	%	No.	%	No.	%
1912	125,761	36,668	29·2	—	—	36,668	29·2
1922	101,377	23,744	23·4	—	—	23,744	23·4
1930	113,552	29,018	25·6	—	—	29,018	25·6
1936	113,448	—[1]	—	—	—	—	—
1956	84,920	31,043	36·5	—	—	31,043	36·5
1957	84,575	29,981	35·4	—	—	29,981	35·4
1958	84,901	28,056	33·0	—	—	28,056	33·0
1959	83,199	27,927	33·6	889	1·0	28,816	34·6
1960	95,241[2]	36,626	38·5	2,223	2·3	38,849	40·8
1961	102,671[2]	41,526	40·4	3,355	3·3	44,881	43·7
1962	104,404	41,696	40·0	4,162	4·0	45,858	44·0
1963	114,067	45,012	39·5	4,473	4·0	49,485	43·5
1964	122,342	47,546	38·8	4,996	4·1	52,542	42·9

[1] No separate figures were given for suspension of prison sentences and suspension of fines.
[2] Sentences for contraventions of the 5th class other than those under Article 40 of the French Penal Code were not included in this figure.

Table 3. Suspension of Imprisonment before the Juvenile Courts

	Total prison sentences	Suspended prison sentences	
		No.	%
1956	771	516	66·9
1957	902	580	64·3
1958	1,486	1,003	67·5
1959	1,747	1,142	65·4
1960	2,615	1,702	65·4
1961	4,112	2,852	69·4
1962	5,290	3,478	65·7
1963	5,533	3,999	72·2
1964	6,820	5,055	74·1

Table 4. Suspension of Fines
(Courts of Summary Jurisdiction, Appeal Courts and Police Courts)

Year	Total fines	Suspended fines	
		No.	%
1909	88,491	38,112	43·1
1912	97,217	36,668	37·7
1922	97,824	37,221	38·0
1930	108,313	46,963	43·3
1956	105,101	17,909	17·0
1957	108,320	17,363	16·0
1958	111,120	17,300	15·6
1959	101,166	11,805	11·7
1960	148,690[1]	10,968	7·4
1961	159,396[1]	12,031	7·5
1962	173,400	10,798	6·2
1963	177,596	11,093	6·2
1964	188,714	10,660	5·6

[1] Contraventions of the 5th class, other than those under Article 40 of the French Penal Code are not included in this figure.

STATISTICAL APPENDIX

Table 5. Regional Variations in the Application of Suspended Sentence (1964)

Large towns	Prison sentences	Suspensions No.	%	Other towns coming under the jurisdiction of the same Appeal Court	Prison sentences	Suspensions No.	%
Paris	21,471	6,796	31·6	Troyes-Chartres Chalons-sur-Marne Rheims Fontainebleau Meaux-Melun Corbeil Pontoise Versailles Auxerre-Sens	10,148	4,807	47·4
Lyons	2,957	1,018	34·4	Belley-Bourg Montbrisson Roanne Saint-Etienne Villefranche-sur-Saône	1,535	640	41·7
Marseilles Nice Toulon	2,951 1,102 710	829 353 245	28·0 32·0 34·1	Digne-Grasse Aix-Tarascon Draguignan	3,131	1,386	44·3
Metz Strasbourg	2,365	568	24·0	Sarreguemines Thionville Saverne-Colmar	2,156	812	37·6
Lille	2,975	1,332	44·8	Avesnes-Cambrai Douai Dunkerque Hazebrouk Valenciennes	4,005	2,020	50·4
Rouen	1,843	737	39·9	Bernay-Evreux Dieppe Le Havre	2,222	1,134	51·0

Table 6(A). Analysis of Suspended Sentence and Probation according to type of Offence
(Courts of Summary Jurisdiction and Appeal Courts)

	Offence against Public Decency					Unintentional wounding					Intentional Assault and Battery				
Year	Total imprison-ments	Ordinary suspended sentences	%	Pro-bations	%	Total imprison-ments	Ordinary suspended sentences	%	Pro-bations	%	Total imprison-ments	Ordinary suspended sentences	%	Probations	%
1956	3,153	1,599	50·7	—	—	2,242	1,537	68·5	—	—	8,380	3,617	43·2	—	43·2
1957	3,056	1,528	30·6	—	—	2,321	1,560	67·2	—	—	8,367	3,458	41·3	—	41·3
1958	2,730	1,397	51·2	—	—	2,248	1,511	67·2	—	—	7,467	3,054	40·9	—	40·9
1959	2,682	1,355	50·5	63	2·3	1,572	1,000	63·6	8	0·5	4,961	2,125	42·8	34	0·7	43·5
1960	2,948	1,608	54·5	110	3·7	1,762[1]	1,226[1]	69·6	22	1·2	5,323[1]	2,475[1]	46·5	119	2·2	48·7
1961	3,457	1,981	57·3	160	4·6	2,022	1,410	69·7	20	1·0	5,819	2,777	47·7	111	1·9	49·6
1962	3,237	1,794	55·4	189	5·8	2,142	2,423	66·4	32	1·5	5,882	2,739	46·6	165	2·8	49·5
1963	3,455	1,884	54·5	217	6·3	2,284	1,527	66·8	32	1·4	6,568	2,869	43·7	182	2·8	46·5
1964	3,412	1,782	52·2	267	7·8	2,547	1,707	67·0	46	1·8	7,174	3,206	44·7	227	3·2	48·0

[1] This figure includes contraventions of the 5th class.

Table 6 (B)

Year	Desertion of family					Larceny				
	Total imprisonments	Ordinary suspended sentences	%	Probations	%	Total imprisonments	Ordinary suspended sentences	%	Probations	%
1956	4,472	1,900	42·5	—	—	27,956	10,364	37·1	—	—
1957	3,997	1,600	40·0	—	—	28,340	10,357	36·5	—	—
1958	3,824	1,487	38·9	—	—	29,245	10,234	35·0	—	—
1959	4,048	1,803	44·5	66	1·6	28,849	9,768	33·9	493	1·7
1960	4,729	2,547	59·8	216	4·6	33,398	11,859	35·5	1,186	3·6
1961	5,653	2,629	46·5	559	9·9	34,638	12,869	37·1	1,643	4·7
1962	5,189	2,319	44·7	584	11·2	36,975	13,541	36·6	1,996	5·4
1963	5,178	2,143	41·4	661	12·8	39,458	14,712	37·3	2,039	5·2
1964	4,987	1,955	39·2	723	14·5	40,809	15,337	37·6	2,195	5·4

Table 6 (C)

Year	Obtaining by false pretences					Breach of trust			
	Total imprisonments	Ordinary suspended sentences	%	Probations	%	Total imprisonments	Ordinary suspended sentences	%	Probations	%
1956	2,133	654	30·7	—	—	4,423	1,544	35·1	—	—
1957	2,038	649	31·8	—	—	4,074	1,531	37·6	—	—
1958	1,905	533	28·0	—	—	3,780	1,335	35·3	—	—
1959	1,738	440	25·3	18	1·0	3,125	1,143	36·6	20	0·6
1960	1,771	479	27·0	28	1·6	3,182	1,217	38·2	74	2·3
1961	2,132	602	28·2	52	2·4	3,635	1,449	39·9	98	2·7
1962	1,938	517	26·7	62	3·2	3,854	1,433	37·2	123	3·2
1963	2,032	604	29·7	52	2·6	4,106	1,504	36·6	135	3·3
1964	2,211	660	29·9	63	2·8	4,831	1,642	34·0	176	3·6

Table 6 (D)

	Dishonoured cheques				Vagrancy and begging					Driving under the influence of drink				
Year	Total imprison-ments	Ordinary suspended sentences	%	Pro-bations	%	Total imprison-ments	Ordinary suspended sentences	%	Pro-bations	%	Total imprison-ments	Ordinary suspended sentences	%	Pro-bations	%
1956	2,940	1,199	40·8	—	—	4,835	225	4·6	—	—	—	—	—	—	—
1957	3,110	1,346	43·3	—	—	5,307	189	3·6	—	—	—	—	—	—	—
1958	3,257	1,464	45·0	—	—	6,025	246	4·0	—	—	—	—	—	—	—
1959	2,878	1,263	43·9	14	0·5	6,541	376	5·7	5	0·1	3,797	2,103	55·4	48	1·3
1960	2,997	1,389	46·3	48	1·6	5,398	274	5·0	25	0·5	8,484	5,273	62·1	139	1·6
1961	3,873	1,892	48·9	48	1·2	3,648	183	5·0	29	0·8	9,819	6,014	61·2	229	2·3
1962	4,402	2,012	45·7	98	2·2	4,233	149	3·5	22	0·5	10,444	6,428	61·5	339	3·2
1963	4,914	2,207	44·9	130	2·6	4,887	173	3·5	23	0·5	12,304	7,115	57·8	486	3·9
1964	6,115	2,383	42·2	141	2·3	4,870	158	3·2	33	0·7	12,998	7,307	56·2	501	3·9

Table 7. Analysis of Suspension according to Length of Prison Sentence
(Courts of Summary Jurisdiction and Appeal Courts)

Year	Total of suspended prison sentences	3 months or less	%	More than 3 months and less than 1 year	%	More than 1 year	%
1912	20,761	18,079	87·1	2,589	12·5	93	0·4
1922	23,744	19,797	83·4	3,794	16·0	153	0·6
1930	29,018	23,273	80·2	5,564	19·2	181	0·6
1964	47,029	38,510	81·9	7,174	15·3	1,345	2·8

Table 8. Analysis of Suspended and Unsuspended Prison Sentences according to Sex

(Courts of Summary Jurisdiction and Appeal Courts)

Year	MALE						FEMALE						Total suspended sentences + probations	
	Total imprisonments	Ordinary suspended sentences	%	Probations	%		Total imprisonments	Ordinary suspended sentences	%	Probations	%		Male	Female
1956	73,310	25,004	34·1	—	—		11,568	6,030	52·1	—	—		34·1	52·1
1957	74,423	24,656	33·1	—	—		10,125	5,321	52·5	—	—		33·1	52·5
1958	75,268	22,979	30·5	—	—		9,616	5,075	52·7	—	—		30·5	52·7
1959	75,027	23,528	31·3	792	1·0		8,172	4,399	53·8	97	1·1		32·3	53·9
1960	85,602	30,934	36·1	2,034	2·3		8,734	5,270	60·3	188	3·5		38·4	63·8
1961	91,179	34,555	37·8	3,047	3·3		10,223	6,558	64·1	308	4·6		41·2	68·7
1962	92,552	34,649	37·4	3,752	4·0		10,542	6,602	62·6	407	6·1		49·4	68·7
1963	100,843	37,031	36·7	4,066	4·0		11,843	7,542	63·6	407	5·3		40·7	68·9
1964	106,546	38,600	36·2	4,478	4·2		13,168	6,429	48·8	518	8·0		40·4	56·8

Table 9. Suspension and Probation according to Age
(Courts of Summary Jurisdiction and Appeal Courts)

Year	Under 20 years					20–30 years					30–40 years					40–60 years					Over 60 years				
	Total	Suspended sentences	%	Probations	%	T.	S.	%	P.	%	T.	S.	%	P.	%	T.	S.	%	P.	%	T.	S.	%	P.	%
1912																									
1922					The categories were different (under 18, 18–21, over 21)																				
1930																									
1936																									
1956	5,277	3,032	57·5	—	—	30,727	11,119	36·2	—	—	21,839	7,345	33·6	—	—	24,277	8,309	34·2	—	—	2,571	1,156	45·0	—	—
1957	6,458	3,626	56·1	—	—	31,266	10,195	34·5	—	—	21,875	7,075	32·3	—	—	22,385	7,373	32·9	—	—	2,464	1,108	45·0	—	—
1958	6,651	3,475	52·2	—	—	32,482	10,142	31·2	—	—	22,851	7,899	34·6	—	—	20,515	6,506	31·7	—	—	2,325	1,032	44·4	—	—
1959	6,350	3,260	51·3	271	4·3	31,951	9,997	31·3	3,253	3·3	23,135	7,095	30·7	151	0·7	19,493	6,635	34·0	133	0·7	2,270	940	41·4	8	0·4
1960	7,464	3,461	46·4	765	10·2	35,274	12,622	35·8	780	6·2	27,606	10,194	36·9	403	3·9	21,463	8,813	41·1	243	1·1	2,529	1,224	48·4	31	1·2
1961	8,140	3,878	47·6	1,023	12·6	36,264	13,758	37·9	1,117	8·1	30,457	11,706	38·4	745	6·3	23,555	10,019	43·3	447	1·9	2,802	1,515	54·1	25	0·9
1962	9,535	4,390	46·0	1,250	13·1	35,593	13,524	38·0	1,337	9·9	30,691	11,516	37·5	960	8·3	24,269	10,187	42·0	560	2·3	2,843	1,573	55·3	44	1·5
1963	10,041	4,830	48·1	1,159	11·5	39,590	14,761	37·3	1,513	10·2	33,755	12,620	37·4	1,066	8·4	26,325	10,821	41·1	683	2·6	2,819	1,534	54·4	46	1·6
1964	10,272	4,853	47·2	1,242	12·1	42,800	15,510	36·2	1,649	10·6	35,636	13,240	37·2	1,170	8·8	27,706	11,658	42·1	746	2·7	3,218	1,739	54·0	33	1·0

Table 10. Prison Convictions according to Age and Sex (year 1904)
(Courts of Summary Jurisdiction and Appeal Courts)

Age group	Male						Female						Total convictions				
	Total imprisonments	Ordinary suspended sentences	%	Probations	%		Total imprisonments	Ordinary suspended sentences	%	Probations	%		Total imprisonments	Ordinary suspended sentences	%	Probations	%
18 to 19	5,325	2,562	48·1	769	14·4		441	287	65·0	54	12·2		5,766	2,849	49·4	823	14·2
19 to 20	3,931	1,675	42·0	366	9·1		525	329	62·6	53	10·0		4,506	2,004	44·4	419	9·2
20 to 21	3,271	1,179	36·0	202	6·1		437	279	63·8	38	8·6		3,708	1,458	39·3	240	6·4
21 to 22	3,676	1,296	35·2	233	6·3		427	263	63·5	20	4·6		4,093	1,559	38·0	253	6·1
22 to 23	3,997	1,378	34·4	196	4·9		373	227	60·8	19	5·0		4,370	1,605	36·7	215	4·9
23 to 24	3,960	1,363	34·4	170	4·2		376	225	59·8	12	3·1		4,336	1,588	36·6	182	4·1
24 to 25	4,031	1,345	33·3	157	3·8		421	257	61·0	24	5·7		4,452	1,602	95·9	181	4·0
25 to 26	3,979	1,273	31·9	144	3·6		403	249	61·7	18	4·4		4,382	1,522	94·7	162	3·6
26 to 27	3,942	1,305	33·1	121	3·0		376	244	64·8	17	4·5		4,318	1,549	35·8	138	3·1
27 to 28	4,101	1,326	32·3	156	3·8		396	269	67·9	14	3·5		4,497	1,595	35·4	170	3·7
28 to 29	4,060	1,329	32·7	128	3·1		343	203	59·1	16	4·6		4,403	1,532	34·7	144	3·7
29 to 30	3,839	1,231	32·0	102	2·6		402	269	66·9	15	3·7		4,241	1,500	35·3	117	2·7
30 to 31	3,904	1,253	32·0	106	2·7		384	250	65·1	9	2·3		4,288	1,503	35·0	115	2·6
31 to 32	3,729	1,232	33·0	123	3·2		384	252	65·6	11	2·8		4,113	1,484	36·0	134	3·2
32 to 33	3,681	1,234	33·5	124	3·3		393	257	65·3	11	2·7		4,074	1,491	36·5	135	3·3
33 to 34	3,699	1,268	34·2	114	3·0		437	264	60·4	16	3·6		4,136	1,532	37·0	130	3·1
34 to 35	3,391	1,147	33·8	107	3·1		382	255	66·7	11	4·1		3,773	1,402	37·1	133	3·2
35 to 36	3,043	1,055	34·6	94	3·0		344	230	66·8	11	3·1		3,385	1,285	37·9	105	3·1
36 to 37	2,865	975	34·0	121	4·2		354	214	60·4	18	5·0		3,219	1,189	36·9	139	4·3
37 to 38	2,577	890	34·5	76	2·9		383	254	66·3	22	5·7		2,960	1,144	38·6	98	3·3
38 to 39	2,505	904	36·0	80	3·1		345	208	60·2	10	2·8		2,850	1,112	39·0	90	3·1
39 to 40	2,481	897	36·1	87	3·5		351	201	59·8	14	3·9		2,832	1,098	38·7	101	3·5
40 to 45	9,604	3,555	37·0	297	3·0		1,477	948	64·1	38	2·5		10,552	4,503	42·6	335	3·1
45 to 50	5,214	1,963	37·6	147	2·8		905	571	63·0	13	1·4		5,785	2,534	43·8	160	2·7
50 to 55	5,540	2,190	39·5	152	2·7		901	571	63·3	16	1·7		6,111	2,761	45·1	168	2·7
55 to 60	3,475	1,450	41·7	76	2·1		410	285	69·4	7	1·1		3,885	1,860	47·8	83	2·1
60 and over	2,615	1,308	50·0	27	1·0		431	308	71·4	6	0·9		3,046	1,739	57·0	33	1·0

Table 11. Analysis by previous Record of Persons granted Suspension with 'mise à l'épreuve'

Year	Total of imprisonment with suspension and mise à l'épreuve	First offenders	%	Previously given suspended sentences	%	Previously remanded in custody	%
1959	881	589	66·8	185	21·0	107	12·2
1960	2,156	1,754	81·3	221	10·3	181	8·4
1961	3,730	2,876	77·1	501	13·4	353	9·5
1962	4,427	3,035	68·6	932	21·0	460	10·4
1963	4,781	3,052	63·8	1,168	24·4	561	11·8
1964	5,319	3,310	62·2	1,397	26·3	612	11·5
1965	6,689	3,972	59·4	1,904	28·4	813	12·2
1966	7,770	5,321	68·5	1,604	20·6	845	10·9

STATISTICAL APPENDIX

Table 12. Suspended Prison Sentences Revoked
(Courts of Summary Jurisdiction and Appeal Courts)

Year	Convictions with suspended prison sentences	Total revoked No.	%	Year of conviction No.	%	2nd year No.	%	3rd year No.	%	4th year No.	%	5th year No.	%	6th year No.	%
								Time at which suspension was revoked							
1902	36,874	3,304	8·9	879	26·6	1,057	32·0	545	16·5	399	12·1	271	8·2	153	4·6
1903	36,669	3,430	9·3	965	28·1	1,069	31·2	600	17·5	392	11·4	259	7·6	145	4·2
1904	37,795	3,509	9·2	844	24·1	1,174	33·5	638	18·2	436	12·4	288	8·2	129	3·6
1908	22,570	2,964	13·1	746	25·2	821	27·7	629	21·2	409	13·8	263	8·9	97	3·2
1922	23,744	1,620	6·8	432	26·7	561	34·6	315	19·5	148	9·1	125	7·7	39	2·4

Table 13. Yugoslavia

Year	Prison sentences	Conditional sentences	%
1960	61,542	34,093	55·4
1961	65,628	38,421	61·3
1962	66,164	38,085	57·5
1963	64,470	41,013	63·6
1964	60,827	37,367	61·0

Table 14. Poland

Year	Percentage of suspensions granted out of total of prison sentences of two years or less
1952	32·7
1953	33·0
1954	48·6
1955	47·3
1961	54·4
1962	55·0
1963	55·7

Table 15. Japan

Year	Total of sentences to solitary confinement and long-term imprisonment[1]	With suspension	%
1928	28,542	4,790	16·3
1929	29,705	5,125	17·1
1930	34,663	5,735	16·5
1931	35,176	6,156	17·5
1932	38,286	6,154	16·1

Year	Solitary confinement and long-term imprisonment[1]	With ordinary suspended sentence or probation	%
1956	101,967	48,789	47·8
1958	92,150	43,228	46·9
1960	88,424	44,573	50·4
1961	82,866	44,197	53·3
1962	80,428	42,536	52·9
1963	76,218	39,983	52·5
1964	73,674	39,529	53·7
1965	78,527	43,336	55·2

[1] 'Solitary confinement' is the punishment of deprivation of liberty for common-law crimes and offences and 'imprisonment' relates to political offences and imprudent acts.

Table 16. Belgium

Year	Total prison sentences	Unsuspended prison sentences		Imprisonment with ordinary suspension	
			%		%
1912	21,327	16,476	77·25	4,851	22·75
1922	14,244	8,946	62·81	5,298	37·19
1930	14,904	10,965	73·57	9,939	26·43
1936	13,870	9,635	69·47	4,235	30·53
1956	16,873	8,668	51·37	8,205	48·63
1957	16,688	8,371	50·16	8,317	49·84
1958	17,475	9,155	52·39	8,320	47·61
1959	17,860	8,806	49·31	9,054	50·69
1960	18,434	9,055	49·12	9,379	50·88
1961	18,296	8,615	47·09	9,681	52·91
1962	16,989	7,680	45·21	9,309	54·79
1963	17,196	7,899	45·94	9,297	54·06
1964	22,281	11,325	50·83	10,956[1]	49·17

[1] The figure for 1964 includes also some awards of probationary suspension. (The law on probation came into force in Belgium on 1st September 1964.) These statistics are for the Courts of Summary Jurisdiction.

Table 17. Greece

Year	Total of sentences of deprivation of liberty	Suspended prison sentences	
			%
1964	76,790	8,721	11·3
1965	80,997	10,983	13·5
1966	102,792	12,461	12·1

Table 18. Italy

Year	Total imprisonments	Suspended prison sentences No.	%
1962	80,727	38,294	47·4
1963	61,003	23,098	37·9
1964	68,264	30,888	45·2

Table 19. Egypt

Year	Suspended sentences	%	Total prison sentences
1958	36,267	32·2	112,536
1959	27,879	21·5	129,571
1960	17,818	11·6	153,308
1961	48,321	28·8	167,814
1962	37,745	22·4	168,695
1963	39,333	23·5	167,482
1964	36,619	27·9	131,161
1965	38,393	27·3	140,538

Table 20. Israel

	Probation				Suspended sentence				Total of sentences			
	1960	1961	1962	1963	1960	1961	1962	1963	1960	1961	1962	1963
Adults	499	483	809	768	5,783	6,036	6,339	5,698	41,985	42,361	48,425	48,151
(percentage)	1·2	1·1	1·7	1·6	13·82	14·2	13·1	11·8				
Juveniles	670	728	861	766	158	211	194	264	5,242	5,126	5,495	5,081
(percentage)	13·0	14·2	15·7	15·1	3·0	4·1	3·5	5·2				
Total	1,178	1,211	1,670	1,534	5,941	6,247	6,533	5,962	47,227	47,487	53,920	53,232
(percentage)	2·5	2·6	3·1	2·9	12·6	13·1	12·1	11·2				

STATISTICAL APPENDIX 93

1. **Suspended Prison Sentences according to type of Offence**
(Courts of Appeal and Courts of Summary Jurisdiction)

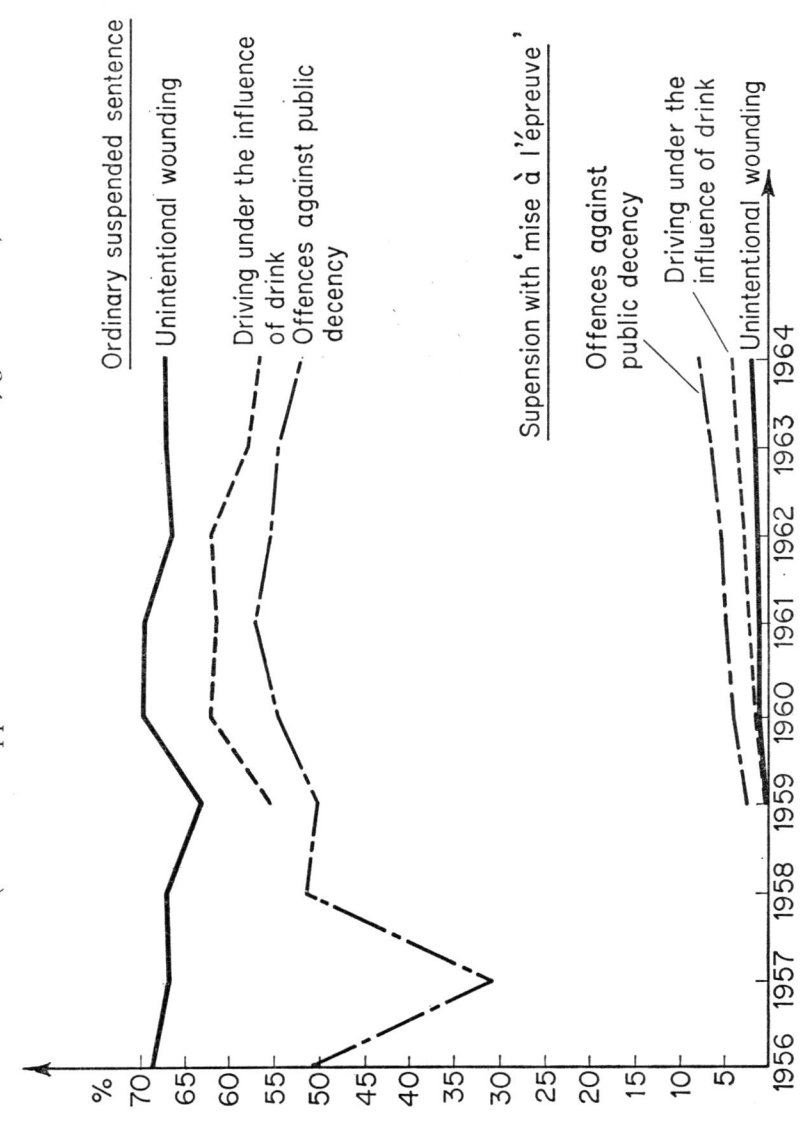

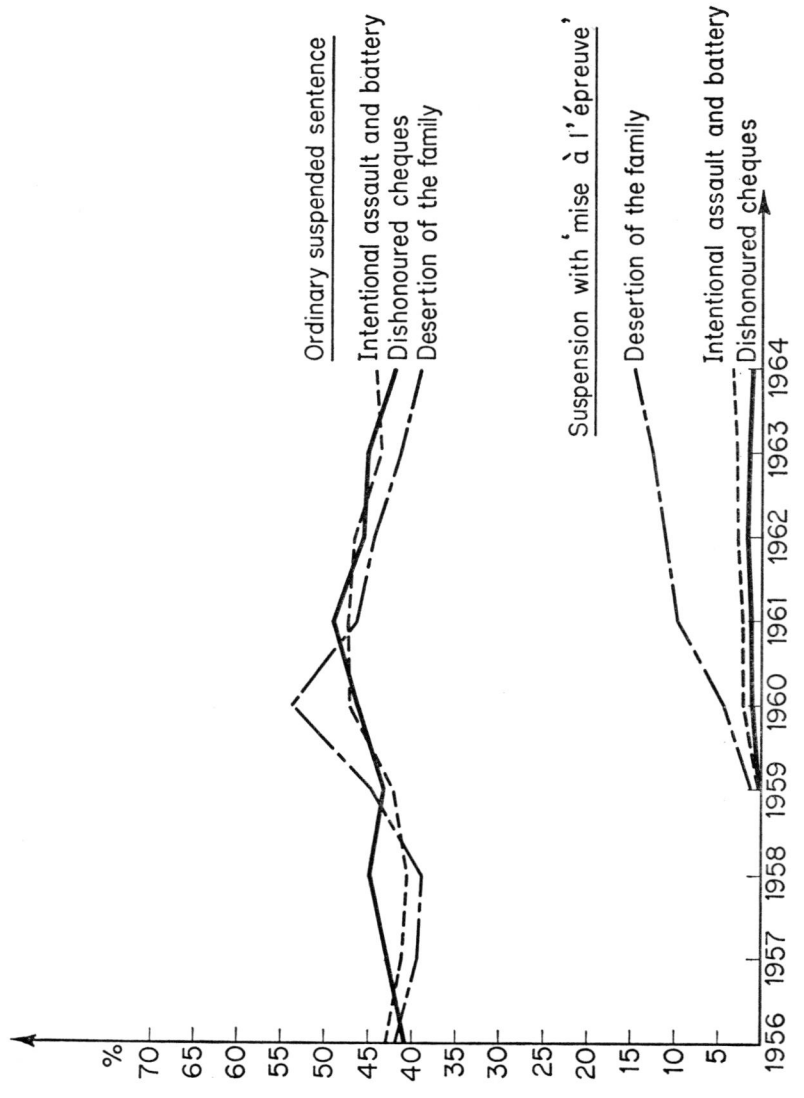

2. **Suspended Prison Sentences according to type of Offence**
(Appeal Courts and Courts of Summary Jurisdiction)

3. Suspended Prison Sentences according to type of Offence
(Appeal Courts and Courts of Summary Jurisdiction)

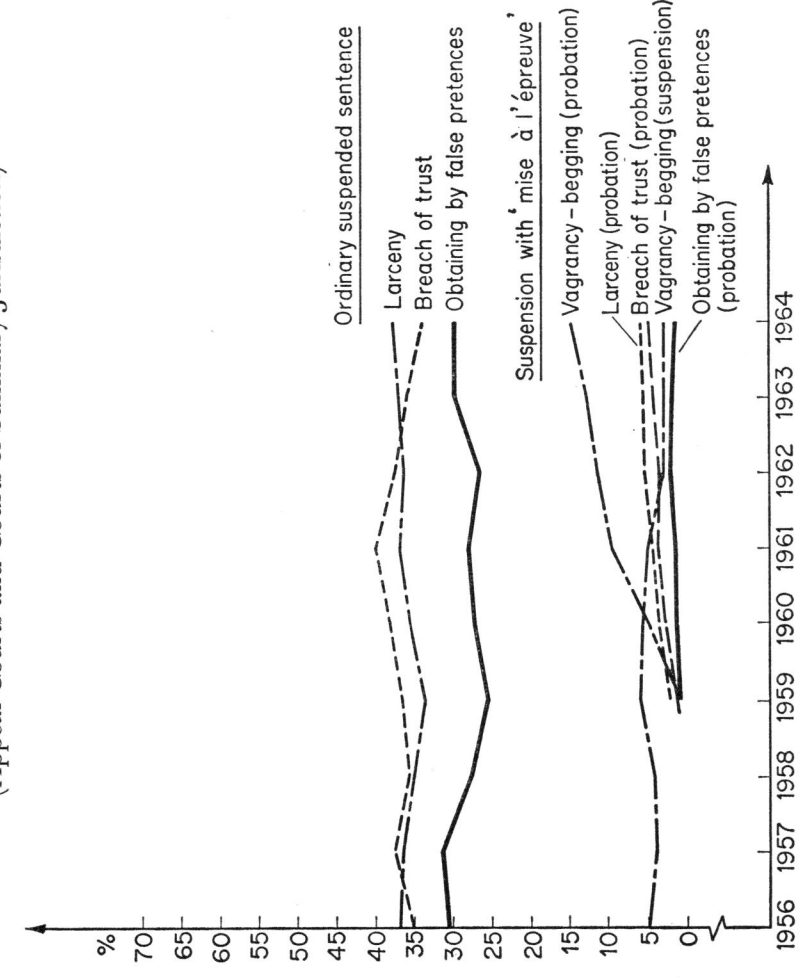

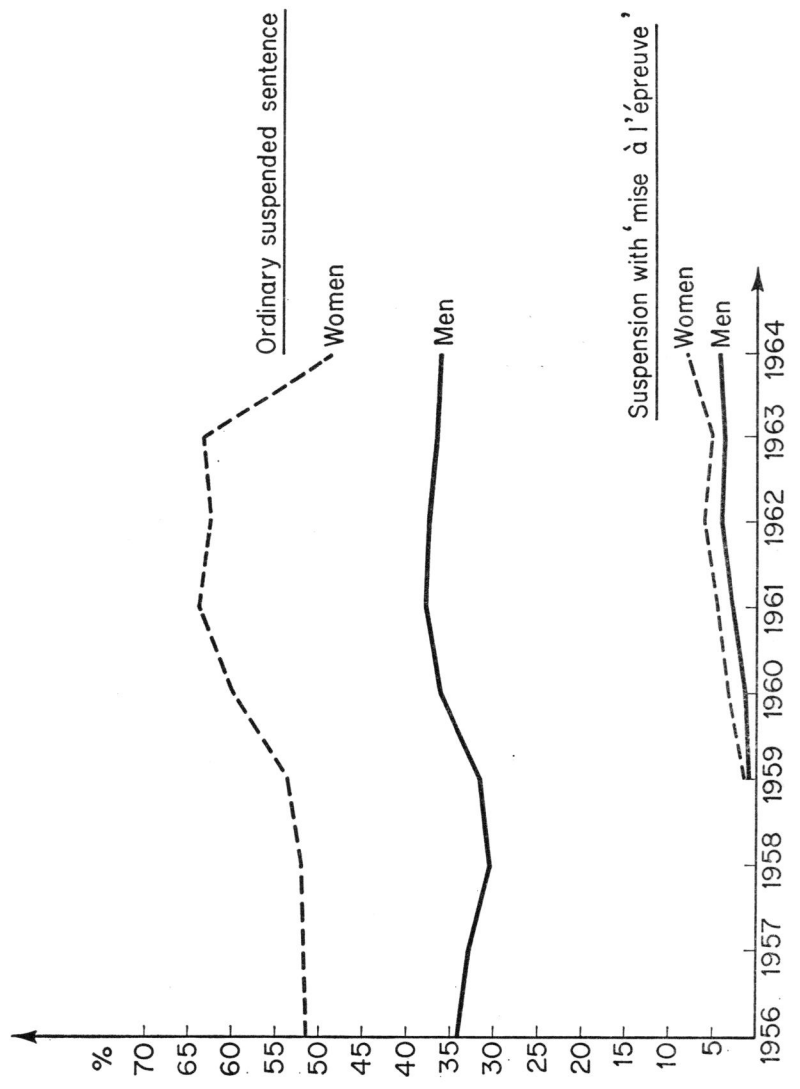

4. Suspended Prison Sentences according to Sex
(Appeal Courts and Courts of Summary Jurisdiction)

STATISTICAL APPENDIX 97

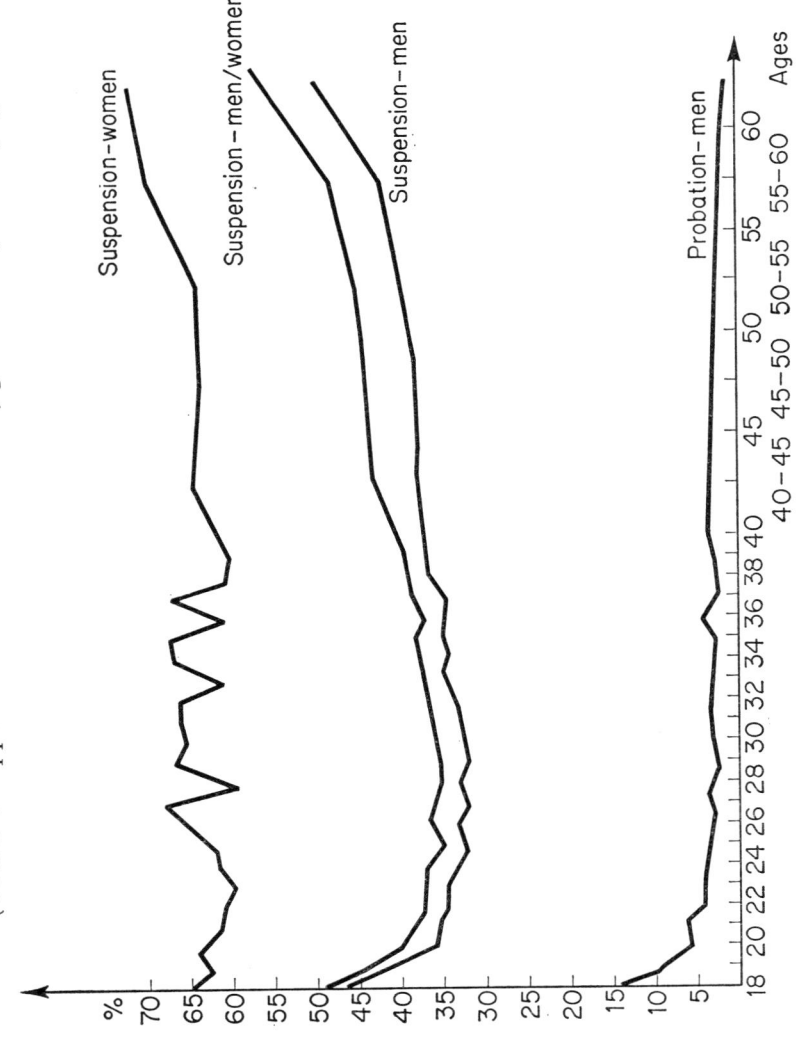

5. Suspended Prison Sentences according to Age and Sex
(Courts of Appeal and Courts of Summary Jurisdiction, Year 1964)

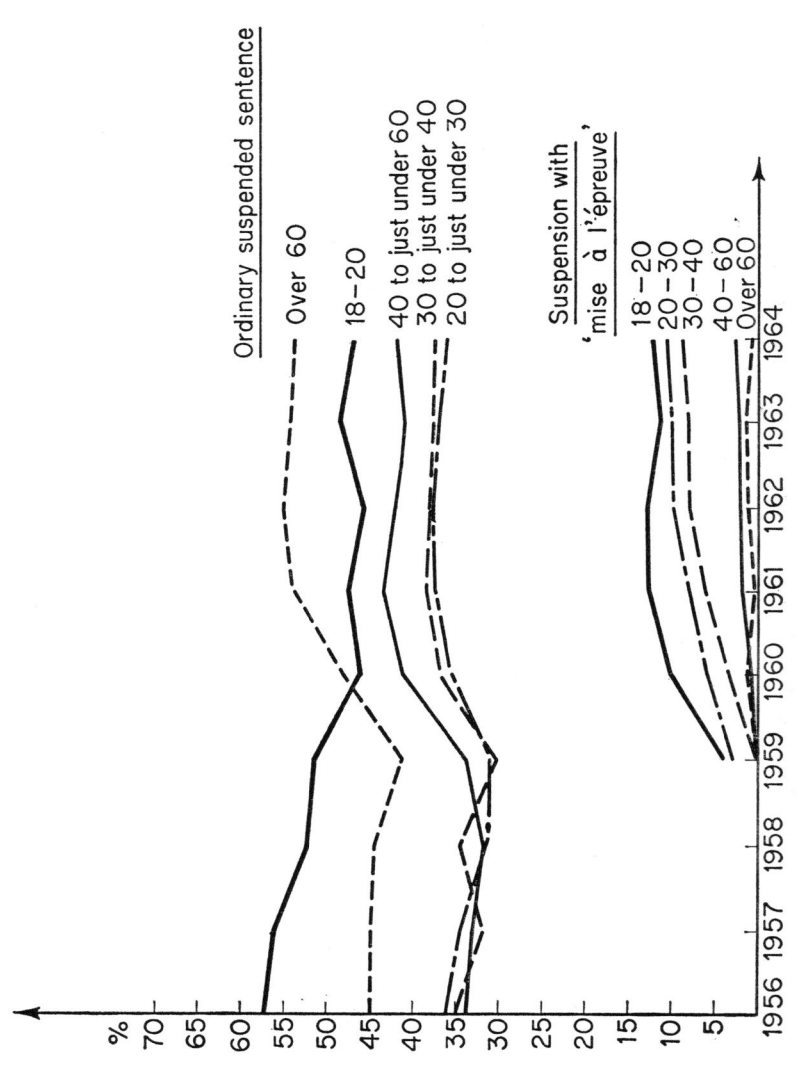

6. Suspended Prison Sentences according to Age
(Appeal Courts and Courts of Summary Jurisdiction)

STATISTICAL APPENDIX

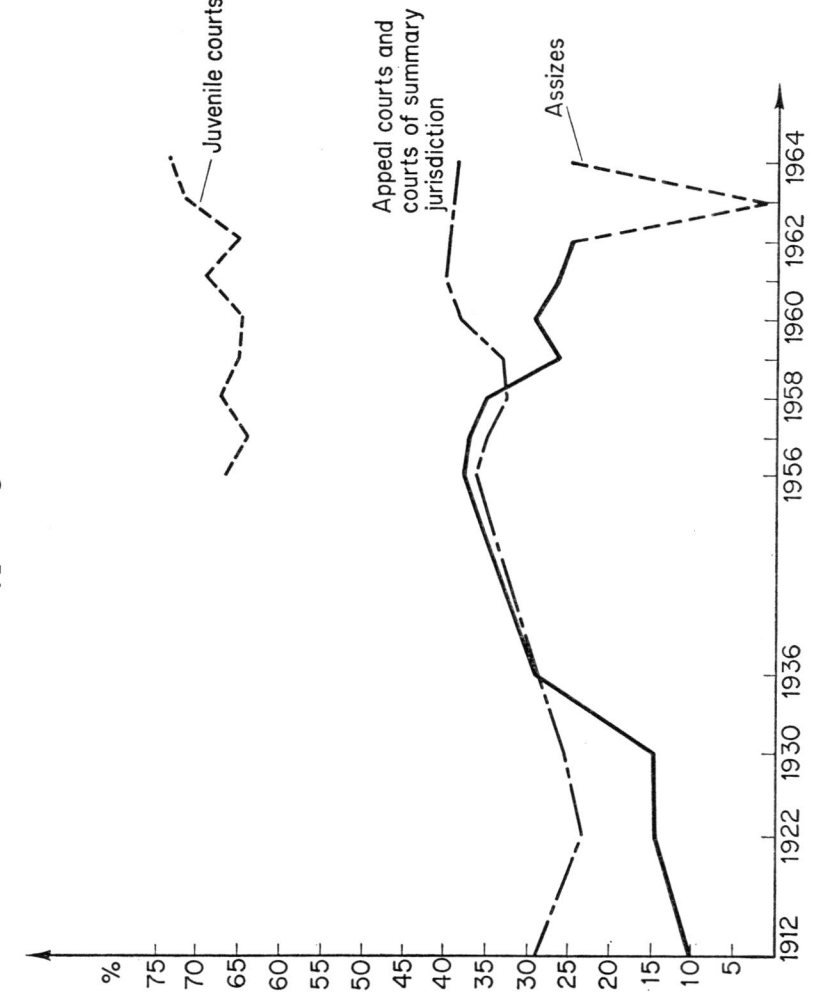

7. Suspended Prison Sentences according to the type of Jurisdiction

Index

Admonition, 2, 9, 30n
African Penal Codes, 38
Age, of offenders, 57-8, 64
Alternative sentence, 6, 8
Ancien regime, law of, 2, 5
Anttila, Inkeri, 61
Appeal courts, 29, 30
Argentina, 40, 51
Argentinian Penal Code, 1922, 29
Asseurement, 3
Austria, draft bill, 1889, 13
Austrian laws, 1952, 29

Beccaria, Cesare Marchese de, 8, 11, 19
Belgium, suspended sentences in, 13, 14, 15, 61
Bentham, Jeremy, 19, 20
Bérenger, Rene, 9, 11, 13, 17, 18, 19, 23, 26, 28, 29n, 30n, 31n, 32, 33n, 35, 65, 66, 69
Bérenger's law, 1, 4, 13, 14, 15, 16, 17, 38, 48, 54
Boitard, 30, 33
Brazil, 40
Brazilian Penal Code, 43
Bulgaria, 39
Bulgarian Penal Code, 1968, 43

Cameroons, 40
Cameroons Penal Code, 38
Carrara, 21, 22
Censura, 2
Chile, 40, 42
Chilean Penal Code 1906, 29
Civil law countries, 66, 70
Colombia, 40
Common law countries, 70
Conditional release, 9-10; in France, 16
Conditional sentence, 1, 20; definition, 15-16; effects, 32; origins, ix

Correia, Eduardo, 44, 47
Costa Rica, 40
Council of Europe, 41
Cuba, 40
Czechoslovakia, 40

de Marsagny, Bonville, 3
Ducpétiaux, 10

East German Code 1968, 43
Ecuador, 40
Egypt, 40; restricted use in, 61; statistics, 91
Egyptian Code, 1904, 25, 29
Establissments de St Louis, 3
Eyschen, 38

Ferri, 16, 18
Fines, excluded or included, 46-7
Finland, 39, 61
First offenders, 6, 7, 27, 38, 43, 67
France, different jurisdictions, in, 53-6; survey of three tribunaux correctionnels, 62; suspended sentence in, ix
French law, 1891, 2
French Penal Code, 1791, 21
Franco-Belgian system, 25-6

Garafalo, 9, 11
German Penal Code, 1871, 13
Germany, reprimand in, 13; suspended sentence in, adopted and abolished, 39
Greece, 39; restricted use in, 61
Guatemala, 40

Hungary, 4, 39, 44

Israel, 40, 41, 42, 46, 49; restricted use in, 61
Italian Penal Code, 29, 49
Italy, 39, 61; reprimand in, 13

INDEX

Japan, 40, 60; recent reforms, 42
Judges, powers of, 4–5

Kikkawa, Tsuneo, 60

Lejeune, 23, 28, 35, 65, 66, 69
Lejeune law, 1, 4, 14, 38
Letters of favour, 3; abolition, 21
L'individualisation de la peine, 12
Liszt, Franz, 39
Lucas, Charles, 10
Luxembourg, 38, 43

Massachusetts, probation in 1869, 14
Mexico, 40
Minors, 45, 52, 58
Mise à l'épreuve, 38, 40, 41, 58, 59, 65, 71; definition, x
Monitio, 2

Netherlands, 39, 42
Northern Ireland, 39, 42, 51
Norway, 39, 45

Operational period, 48
Osborough, Nial, 40*n*

Panama, 40
Pardon, power of, infringed, 22
Peru, 40
Poland, 45, 59, 60; statistics, 88
Police supervision, 24
Polish law, rules out suspended sentences, 25
Polish Penal Code, 40, 44
Portugal, 38, 41, 42
Portuguese Penal Code, 14, 29
Prison, in French Legal System, 5
Probation, ix, x, 14, 34, 66; in Britain, 14; in France, 59, 64; in Massachusetts, 14; in New Zealand, 14; with second suspended sentence, 50
Prostitution, 46

Recidivism, 7, 10, 11, 14, 16, 28, 31, 61, 63
Recognizance, 4, 66

Recorded sentence, 39
Rehabilitation, 6
Remand in custody, 57
Reprimand, 2; in Germany and Italy, 13; in Portugal, Russia, and Switzerland, 14
Resolutory condition, 35
Restitution as condition, 49
Revocation, 50; automatic, 36; statistics, 87
Rossi, on imprisonment, 8
Rumania, 40, 51
Rumanian Code, 44
Russia, 40, 44

Saleilles, 12, 24
Salvador, 40
Sardinian Penal Code, 2
Schönborn, Count, 13
Senegal, suspended sentence conditional in, 25
Sentences, increases with suspension, 67; length of, 45, 56, 82; pronouncement of, 30, 32, 34; short, 11
Severa interlocutio, 2*n*
Sex of offenders, 57, 58, 64, 85
Spain, 39, 46, 49, 61
Stoos, Carl, 22
Strafaussetzung zur Bewährung, 61
Supervision of offenders, 24
Suspended sentences (*See also* Conditional sentence): abolition or suspension of, 24–5; alternative procedures, 69; application, 51; basic principles, 20; conceptions of, 35; conditions imposed, 25, 49; in countries other than France, 59; definition, ix; disuse, in Russia, 42; draft bill 1884, 16; early beginnings, 6; effects, 51; effectiveness, 61; as favour and as treatment, 69; granting of, 49; immediate background, 13; offenders eligible for, 27; opposition to, 66–7; origins, 1; partial, in Denmark, 47; present systems, 41; and probation system, 66, 68, 70; procedure in grant of, 28; proportions of, 59–61; refusal

of, 68; significance, 65; as special legal institution, 22; technique, 43; time limits, 33, 34; uses by different jurisdictions, 53
Suspension of imposition of sentence, 42
Sweden, 39, 49; early suspended sentences in, 4
Swedish Penal Code, ix, 42, 71
Swiss Penal Code, 29, 42, 43, 44
Switzerland, 47

Tickets of leave, 10

Travieu, amendment to Bérenger law, 17
Tripartite system, in France and Belgium, 26
Turkey, 40

Uruguay, 40

Weekend arrest, 69
West Germany, 41, 45, 50, 61

Yugoslavia, 34, 59

Zurich, suspended sentences in, 4

Soc
HV
9354
P3

DATE DUE	
DEC 10 1973	JAN 2 8 1976
FEB 18 1973	MAR 10 1973
DEC 10 1974	
AUG 11 1975	
JUN 4 1979	
B FEB 21 1987	
DEC 17 1997	